PLAYFUL FICTIONS
AND
FICTIONAL PLAYERS

Kennikat Press
National University Publications
Literary Criticism Series

General Editor
John E. Becker
Fairleigh Dickinson University

PLAYFUL FICTIONS
AND
FICTIONAL PLAYERS

Game, Sport, and Survival
in Contemporary American Fiction

NEIL DAVID BERMAN

National University Publications
KENNIKAT PRESS // 1981
Port Washington, N.Y. // London

Manufactured in the United States of America

Published by
Kennikat Press Corp.
Port Washington, N.Y. / London

Library of Congress Cataloging in Publication Data

Berman, Neil David, 1947-
    Playful fictions and fictional players.

    (Literary criticism series) (National university
publications)
    Bibliography: p.
    Includes. index.
    1. American fiction—20th century—History and
criticism. 2. Sports in literature. 3. Plays in
literature. I. Title.
PS374.S76B4   813'.54'09355   80-20230
ISBN 0-8046-9265-3

For Harry and Dorothy,
my favorite players

ACKNOWLEDGMENTS

I would like to thank the editors of *Modern Fiction Studies* and *Critique* for their kind permission to use material which originally appeared, in slightly different form, in those journals. I would also like to thank Jack Higgs, Jim Kincaid, and Tony Libby for their generous suggestions, which have everywhere helped improve and solidify much of my own thinking about sport and literature. To my students at Ohio State University, the University of Hawaii at Hilo, and the United States Naval Academy, I owe a very special debt of gratitude for their encouragement and patience in helping me formulate many of the ideas which, hopefully, inform this book. My greatest debt of all is acknowledged in the dedication.

ACKNOWLEDGMENTS

CONTENTS

PLAYFUL FICTIONS
AND
FICTIONAL PLAYERS

ABOUT THE AUTHOR

Neil David Berman is an assistant professor of
English at the U.S. Naval Academy in Annapolis,
Maryland. He has had a longstanding interest in sports
and in the literature about sports. He is the author
of various articles on American literature.

PLAYFUL FICTIONS and FICTIONAL PLAYERS

Just over a decade ago, René Maheu argued that although there are many significant parallels between sport and culture, sport is almost absent as a theme in cultural works. "In philosophy, literature, the theatre, even the cinema, in painting, sculpture, and music, works of merit based on sport either in form or substance are few indeed. It inspires only a very small number of works of the mind or of art of any aesthetic significance."[1] As a comment on American literature of the last hundred years, Maheu's statement is simply wrong, but even if one accepts the gist of his criticism, it is astonishing to note how fully the past decade has invalidated it.

Only one year after Maheu's address, Paul Weiss published a major philosophic inquiry into sport and its aesthetics. More recently, Howard S. Slusher and Bernard Suits have written more specialized philosophical studies of sports and games respectively. Suits's book, *The Grasshopper: Games, Life and Utopia*, is itself a playful attempt to invoke the classic form of the Platonic dialogue to analyze a contemporary cultural problem. A number of interesting movies have been released in the last few years: *Visions of Eight, Bang the Drum Slowly, Fat City, North Dallas Forty, Deliverance,* and *The Bad News Bears* (only the first in the series), to name six. All are vast improvements over the sports soap operas produced in the 1940s and 1950s, typified by films like *The Babe Ruth Story*. In sculpture, there is far too much recent work to catalog here, but a look at Benjamin Lowe's *The Beauty of Sport* (1977) will show a real proliferation of serious interest in sport as subject matter. In painting, the

3

work of Leroy Neiman has some aesthetic merit. Nonfictional prose about sports has recently been graced by the contributions of John McPhee, Roger Angell, George Plimpton, Norman Mailer, Roger Kahn, and John Updike. And in the theater, *That Championship Season* won the Pulitzer Prize among a host of other awards.

But perhaps the most striking rebuttal to Maheu's argument is the extraordinary number of recent American novels using sports as a dominant theme. It is no mere coincidence that at least two dozen important sports novels have been written in the past decade, a period which has seen unprecedented growth in the commercial value of sport.[2] Most of these recent novels were written by relatively young writers, and with just a few exceptions, like Philip Roth's *The Great American Novel* and Jerome Charyn's *The Seventh Babe*, most are first or second novels. While sport is certainly an important motif in the work of older American writers like Malamud, Bellow, Warren, and Morris, the fecundity of the last ten or twelve years is really startling. I am not suggesting that serious sports fiction in America is the exclusive province of the young, but that the extraordinary cultural, social, and economic impact of sports has been more acutely felt by the generation of American writers now in their thirties and forties. Younger American novelists, writing about their experience of America, have found in sports both a dynamic metaphor for reality and reality itself.

Any discussion of sports as a theme and metaphor in literature must inevitably confront the problems of the seriousness and reality of play and games as aspects of culture. Huizinga says that play precedes culture, and that the play element permeates all aspects of culture.[3] We are, indeed, just as thoroughly a race of players as we are toolmakers or thinkers. What makes sports fiction so exciting is that it brings man's play nature starkly into focus and forces both the reader and critic to confront more directly than is usual the significance of games and game playing in contemporary culture. In a celebrated article on the ontology of play, Eugen Fink defines play as broadly as Huizinga does:

Play is a basic existential phenomenon, just as primordial and autonomous as death, love, work and struggle for power, but it is *not* bound to these phenomena in a common ultimate purpose. Play, so to speak, confronts them all—it absorbs them by representing them. We play at being serious, we play truth, we play reality, we play work and struggle, we play love and death—and we even play play itself.[4]

Writing from a completely different perspective, the psychologist Erik H. Erikson has found a similarly universal function for play in human experience:

The child's play is the infantile form of the human ability to deal with experience by creating model situations and to master reality by experiment and planning. It is in certain phases of his work that the adult projects past experience into dimensions which seem manageable. In the laboratory, on the stage, and on the drawing board, he relives the past and thus relieves leftover affects; in reconstructing the model situation, he redeems his failures and strengthens his hopes. He anticipates the future from the point of view of a corrected and shared past.[5]

For Erikson play is an essentially re-creative function whose most basic application is in problem solving.

The play of very young children is purely assimilative and often shows little or no awareness of other persons. By playing with the sounds of his voice or the movement of his fingers "the infant is slowly but surely transforming his artful play into the skill of assimilative make-believe. . . . He is readying himself for the playing of games, not simply the playing of play. . . ."[6] Piaget tells us that in the next stage of development (generally from two to seven years old), the child gradually progresses from purely symbolic games to games with rules.[7] Allen Guttmann makes essentially the same point in distinguishing between spontaneous and organized play. While spontaneous play is a paradigm of freedom, "games symbolize the willing surrender of absolute spontaneity for the sake of playful order. One remains outside the sphere of material necessity, but one must obey the rules one imposes on oneself."[8] This marks an important transition in the development of the child, for rules imply at least some degree of regulation and competition, the process by which the child must learn to accommodate himself to external reality.

In the most basic way, then, play is the raw material of games. There are surely as many definitions of games as there are game theorists, but several important characteristics are almost universally accepted. Games imply two or more sides (even if the other player or team is either imaginary or one's previous performance) and thus competition. A game is also play organized by agreed-upon rules. A violation of the rules is also a violation of the spirit of play and thus a profanation of the game itself. Presumably, there are also some criteria for determining the winner of a game. Of course, the concern here is with sports, which are very special kinds of games with intricately structured organizations and rules. One typology of games classifies them into three overlapping groups: games of chance, games of strategy, and games of physical skill. Some games are essentially bounded by only one of the above classifications; chess, for example, is exclusively a game of strategy. Others, like poker, rely on both strategy and chance. One of the compelling features of sports, however, is that they, in various and changing combinations, feature all three of the above categories with special emphasis on highly developed physical skills. Sport is thus the specific manifestation of play which appeals to the broadest spectrum of people as a model for succeeding over others.[9]

The seminal theories of play and its relation to culture, Huizinga's *Homo Ludens* and Caillois's *Man, Play and Games*, are both characterized by several key intellectual oppositions. Jacques Ehrmann has recently summarized the most important of these oppositions as follows: play/ seriousness, gratuitousness/usefulness, sterility/fecundity, leisure/work, literature/science, and unreality/reality.[10] The reader of sports fiction must also confront these same tensions. Is it mere paradox to speak of the reality of the play-sphere? How serious is the world of play? How valid is the dualism that presupposes a tension between work and play?

Huizinga says that although some play may be very serious indeed, its "pretending" quality betrays an inferiority to seriousness.[11] He argues that play begins and ends, moves toward closures, and contains its own course and meaning. This quality of isolation, for Huizinga, also distinguishes play from ordinary life.[12] And yet, implicit in Huizinga's analysis is the idea that, at their best, activities which conform to the play-attitude, such as rituals, duels, even warfare, are very serious indeed. Similarly, Caillois says that although games are absorbing, they develop "in a separate, ideal world, sheltered from any fatal consequence. . . ."[13] In light of the cultural significance of sports in contemporary America, both arguments are naive; for, as Ehrmann says, "play cannot be defined by isolating it on the basis of its relationship to an *a priori* reality and culture. To define play is *at the same time* and *in the same movement* to define reality and to define culture. As each term is a way to apprehend the two others, they are each elaborated, constructed through and on the basis of the two others. None of the three existing prior to the others, they are all simultaneously the subject and the object of the question which they put to us and we to them."[14]

In other words, play, reality, and culture are radically interdependent, and thus properly resist isolation. The idea of a sheltered, safe play-world is completely refuted by American sports fiction. How can the Universal

Baseball Association be considered a safe play-sphere in view of Damon Rutherford's death and the subsequent collapse of Henry Waugh? Failure is a central theme in sports fiction, and it points up the danger of *not* taking the world of the game as both serious and real. We have, in addition to Henry Waugh, Elwood Baskin's psychological breakdown in *One on One*, the personal and financial failures of Ernie Munger and Billy Tully in *Fat City*, Gary Harkness's attempted suicide in *End Zone*, and the tragic failure of love to save the violent world of *North Dallas Forty*.

The natural tendency to think of sports in terms of a dualism defined by the tension between the world of the game and the real world is consistently denied by contemporary sports fiction. It is impossible to consider sports apart from their social consequences, their influence on culture, their ultimate reality, significance, and seriousness, because, as Ehrmann says, "the distinguishing characteristic of reality is that it is played. Play, reality, culture are synonymous and interchangeable. Nature does not exist prior to culture. The role of the critic is specifically to understand and to explain by language (literary language in particular) how this nature-culture manifests itself in different historical and cultural contexts."[15]

The specific historical and cultural context to be considered here is contemporary America. Each of the five writers included in this study portrays contemporary America as a world of vastly limited possibility. Play, often specifically manifested as sport, offers the possibility, real or apparent, of achieving some liberation and hence self-definition, however minimal, in a reductive world. The player seeks escape from an environment he finds uninteresting at best, intolerable at worst. Play is never opposed to reality or seriousness, but each novel *does* suggest a dualism between play (though not always sport) and the modern world; a repressive, technological society is constantly challenging the more liberating values of play.

The true player is an "adventurer," as Robert E. Neale describes him. Mature play may thus imply the risks one takes in leaving the safety of an onerous routine. For Neale, play is any activity not arising out of the need to resolve inner conflict.[16] This psychological definition is certainly in keeping with Huizinga's, for whom play is an eminent manifestation of human freedom. Indeed, freedom is the very first characteristic of human play, for whatever risks he may take, the adventurer acts out of a sense of harmony. The implications of this definition of play for serious sports fiction are extremely significant. A world of minimal possibility is antagonistic to any liberating activity. Therefore the player seeking a free and creative adventure must usually internalize his play in order to exist at all in a repressive environment.

The major and representative novels discussed here vary widely in technique and in some assumptions, but they all share the same startling vision of a world that is actively hostile to any manifestation of freedom, any play. Those forms of play it pretends to allow—sports—it manages to deaden, to transform into a grotesque parody of true play. In order to exist in the modern world, and certainly in order to become a transforming reality, play *must* be internalized. As long as a novelist chooses a naturalistic treatment of sport the very best that can happen is the partial recovery of play. Play can be joined to sport and to personal freedom, then, only insofar as that sport can be imaginatively re-created.

In *Fat City*, a highly naturalistic novel reminiscent of Crane's *Maggie*, play is irrelevant even in potential to the lifestyle of small-time boxers. What seem to be the moments of greatest joy in *Fat City* are moments of deep conflict. Billy Tully and Ernie Munger fight *because* they need money, *because* they need male camaraderie, or *because* they want to escape the painful tedium of farm labor. They never box for the sake of playing, only as a means to another end. Their "play" is always an attempt, more or less unsuccessful, to resolve or escape from some basic conflict and thus not genuine play.

In *North Dallas Forty*, there is some potential for play, but it is never fully realized. Phil Elliott experiences flashes of joy and freedom while catching a football, but these tantalizing glimpses of liberation are constantly undercut and finally destroyed by a repressive society of super-technology. Whereas the player confronts the world directly, *North Dallas Forty* emphasizes the vicarious experience of spectators and trivializes the more important, direct experience that takes place on the field. True play, for the athlete, for the child, for the artist, is an expression of human joy, freedom, and creativity. In *North Dallas Forty*, play cannot be recovered because it is overwhelmed by the antagonistic emphasis on computer technology and indirect experience.

Important differences in the nature of the play-world begin to emerge in *End Zone*. Although the realistic description of the football season is itself very much like that in *North Dallas Forty*, other, more spontaneous and primitive forms of play appear. Play becomes not only possible in *End Zone*, but is partially recovered. Spontaneous games and verbal foreplay which exemplify the essential characteristics of play begin to appear as alternatives to the threatening potential of imminent nuclear holocaust and increasingly abstract language. The novel poses the choice of total submission to the increasingly regimented uses of technology and the encroachments into the creative/communicative potential of language or a harkening back to a more primitive, ritualized past to recover the play-attitude.

Lawrence Shainberg's *One on One* is still another sports novel about the disintegration of modern life and the sterilization of language. Unlike *End Zone*, the imagery here is not of holocaust and nuclear destruction; it is the imagery of fragmentation, of a society no longer cohesive (if it ever was), where individual schizophrenia mirrors a larger cultural breakdown. The vision of the book is psychological; the growing schizophrenia of Elwood Baskin is symptomatic of a larger social psychosis. Elwood himself attributes his illness to basketball, and yet he feels the game itself will help him feel better. The game is thus sickness and cure, dangerous and safe simultaneously. The title image, "one on one," is expressive of noncohesive, individual play in basketball, and is a marvelous metaphor for the world of this novel, where communication and love are minimal and the distinction between reality and fantasy is impossible to decipher.

In that muddling between reality and fantasy lies the significance of *One on One* for this study. For the first time in any of these novels play becomes a truly transforming reality. While visions of Elwood's parents, his psychiatrist, his public relations manager, and his girl friend rage on as absurdly as ever inside his head, Elwood meditates on the transcendent significance of basketball. Unlike Gardner's use of boxing as a metaphor for the individual's painful struggle in a repressive society, basketball in *One on One* becomes a metaphor for art, for the dance, for all the liberating values associated with play. The play-attitude is achieved in *One on One*, not by reaching backward to a more primitive world as in *End Zone*, but by internalizing the modern world, and occasionally transcending it.

It is significant that the more fully the play-attitude is achieved in sports novels, the more closely it is identified with schizophrenia. The player, by internalizing his experience, achieves a reality separate from that of the repressive world of work. In *The Universal Baseball Association*, the low-mimetic world of Henry Waugh's accounting job is constantly being opposed to the more fantastic world of his Association. Waugh can be seen not simply as the "proprietor" of his game, but also as its godlike creator. Indeed, his initials—J. H. W.—identify him with the

Hebrew god Yahweh. He has performed the ultimate creative act—a god-like one—by creating an entire world. In Henry Waugh's world the imagination becomes an end in itself, so compelling as to exclude all other facets of human activity. He lives, eventually, entirely in a world of art, of fabrication, of fantasy. Even some casual sex with a B-girl is only possible through Henry's ability to correlate the metaphors of sex with the images of his baseball game, and his identification with Damon Rutherford, one of the heroes of the game. By the last chapter of the novel, Henry has ceased to appear as a character. He exists only through his identification with the actors in his play-world. Indeed, for Henry, the world of his game has become *the* world. The dreary, naturalistic world of accounting has been completely transcended by play. By presenting a completely internalized play-world with its own myths and rituals, *The Universal Baseball Association* represents a natural climax to this study, an absolute alternative to the self-perpetuating defeatism of *Fat City*. The world of *The Universal Baseball Association* has been so completely internalized that it creates its own myths and rituals, entirely cut off from such established mythic traditions as are employed in Malamud's *The Natural*. The search for a transforming reality may indeed be reached through play, but only play which has been separated and personalized as private myth, art, or religion.

While each writer in this study suggests a dualism between play and a repressive society, none accepts the fact that play is opposed to seriousness, work, or reality. Contemporary sports fiction consistently denies the validity of such dualisms, attacks them as being naive, and collapses them to show how play *is* work, sport *is* reality, and sport *is* serious. It is wrong to think of Henry Waugh's game world as being opposed to the real world because it is itself the real world, and, if anything, makes the world of accounting seem unreal by comparison. Sports fiction is always about reality; only the metaphor the fictional work utilizes to describe reality varies. As Eugen Fink says, "If we define play in the usual manner by contrasting it with work, reality, seriousness, and authenticity, we falsely juxtapose it with other existential phenomena."[17]

Even Johan Huizinga, who presupposes a dualism between play and seriousness or play and work, occasionally equivocates on the problem: "The play-concept as such is of a higher order than is seriousness. For seriousness seeks to exclude play, whereas play can very well include seriousness."[18] How could Huizinga, writing before the age of television, have been anything but naive about the distinction between work and play in sports? He wrote before the era of football widows; professional drafts of college ballplayers; astronomical salaries for professional athletes; legal battles over the infamous reserve clause in baseball, which treats professional athletes as property; the vastly intricate system of little leagues and pee-wee leagues, complete with uniforms, managers, even assistant coaches, all for eight- or nine-year-olds; and, of course, *Monday Night Football.* For the professional, amateur, and college athlete in contemporary America, work is play and play is work.

The dualisms of work/play, play/seriousness, and play/reality must be forgotten if we are to take seriously (the word just cannot be avoided) the alternative, internalized play-worlds established by sports fiction. David Miller has written in *Gods and Games* that "perhaps seriousness and nonseriousness are simply two different ways man has of playing his life, and perhaps for the playful eye of *Homo Ludens* these two ways are finally not all that different. They are both play."[19] Ehrmann has written that even the player may be played.[20] And what better illustration of this is there than Henry Waugh playing with "imaginary" baseball players and Robert Coover, at one remove further, playing with Waugh? Waugh cannot play at his work, so he plays at his game. The working world, if it is automated and dehumanizing enough to prevent one from playing at it, may seem much less real than the games one plays in the park or watches on television. Arnold Beisser, a psychiatrist who has worked closely and extensively with the problems of athletes, argues convincingly that the reality of the game may well be more meaningful than the reality of ordinary work:

The work world which is socially defined as real may not feel that way when it has become superspecialized and seemingly separated from its products. The individual performing a function not in harmony with his biology may do it in a perfunctory manner. The pushbutton world is defined as real but may seem more like a fantasy. Which is more real, a consensually defined abstraction or a game which is more consistent with man's biological nature? The fantasy of the game becomes not a game at all.[21]

Phil Elliott and Henry Waugh vividly illustrate the extremes of Beisser's point. Both men are would-be players struggling for survival in mechanical, reflexive environments which constantly thwart their play instincts. Elliott must conform to the computer technology of a professional football team; Waugh must abide the compulsive work habits of Horace Zifferblatt. The difference between the two is that Elliott remains a part

of the reductive world which stifles the play-attitude. He never successfully internalizes his play and so never takes the "adventure" which
Robert E. Neale says is essential to play. Waugh takes that adventure.
While his accounting work remains "perfunctory," he does internalize,
indeed he fantasizes, his play, and the result is an enormously compelling
adventure.

It seems clear that play, especially as it is internalized, may give the
individual a respite from the confusion of a world of limited possibility.
It may be a means of transcending that world. But of all the metaphors
which embody the play-attitude, why sport? Why not painting, or child's
play, or sex? The athlete and the gamesman surely have affinities with
other players, but the writers in this study have chosen sports as their
major theme because it speaks very directly to their experience of contemporary America.

Sport is the child of a technological society. The tremendous increase
in the economic growth of sports in recent years parallels corresponding
advances in the aviation industry, computer technology, and the communication sciences, especially television. Network television coverage
of college football alone is worth well over $30 million. Distinctions
between amateur and professional have become so ambiguous as to be
almost meaningless. Sports are big business in America today, and the
players, equipment, arenas, and games themselves are all parts of the means
of production. While we may tend to associate sport with leisure and with
values antagonistic to technology, sport tends, especially when it is pro-
fessionalized and promoted, to depersonalize its participants. Ironically,
in doing so, sport often merely changes the individual's confrontation with
one machine for another more pernicious one. We have no better example
of this than the absolute conformity demanded by professional football in *North Dallas Forty*. As Phil Elliott comes to realize, the "game
plan" is the product of computer technology, and the player, in order
to survive, must allow himself to become part of a larger machine.

Although many games require all players to play similar roles—
hopscotch, poker, checkers—athletes are often highly specialized in their
role functions and thus represent the specialization of a sophisticated
technological age. One might argue that singles tennis or bowling or golf
require the full range of skills inherent in those sports. But the big team
sports like football, baseball, basketball, even tennis doubles require very
specialized skills. One could hardly substitute a defensive halfback for a
pulling guard in an emergency situation. Baseball has gone so far as to

institute not only designated hitters, but also, incredibly, designated runners. Late-inning defensive specialists have been part of the game for many years. The athlete, then, may well be a good representative of contemporary consciousness in a culture of superspecialization.

While commercialized sport may indeed pervert the play-attitude, as it surely does in *North Dallas Forty*, the athlete may, with rigor and discipline, attain a degree of perfection through his body which would not otherwise be possible. "To achieve desired goals in sport, demands are placed on man that require voluntary commitment to a world of strenuous discipline and movement. In this way, man, by taking part in a free act, comes to remember his freedom, a freedom his societal form of living has since caused him to negate."[22] The athlete is an expression of what man can achieve through his individual mind and body under particular circumstances. Unlike the painter, for example, "in the athlete all can catch a glimpse of what one might be were one also to operate at the limit of bodily capacity."[23]

One could argue that other forms of play are equally viable metaphors for the individual's striving for perfection in a world of conformity. But the difference is that sport concerns itself with records in a way that makes it more available and decipherable than other forms of play. In a spiritually prosperous age perhaps a Botticelli *Venus* might be a standard of perfection, but in an age of computer technology, in the wake of the "death of god" theologies, there is something comforting about the definiteness and finality of numerical records. Records provide a measure of control and security in a world of vast uncertainty.

The availability of sports to both participants and spectators marks it as a possibility for a new American frontier. Science and medicine require highly academic skills. But the fan, the spectator, and the player all participate directly and vicariously in the crossing of new athletic boundaries. We simply do not identify with scientists or painters in the way we identify with athletes. And one comes to identify with an athlete most specifically and vehemently through records. What obsesses Henry Waugh more than any other aspect of his game is the record keeping. For the exemplary fan it is too often true that without records there is no order to sport; the individual's striving becomes existentially pointless. It is no wonder then that the pivotal incidents in *The Universal Baseball Association* involve Henry Waugh's search for perfection through Damon Rutherford and the tragic denial of that perfection.

An important function of sport, one which is enhanced by our obsession with record keeping, is to "provide for the individual continuity of interest at various ages, in a culture filled with ambiguity of role function."[24] The significance of Damon Rutherford's perfect game is intensified by the fact that he is the son of Brock Rutherford, one of the first great players in the history of the Association. Henry's complete identification with Damon makes plausible his despair after the rookie pitcher's death. By the last chapter of the novel, 101 seasons later, all members of the Association are descendants of older players. The world of the game has been sealed off; it provides its own continuity.

And continuity here implies self-sufficiency. The spectator's fascination with sport has a lot to do with the metaphorical fertility of sports. Murray Ross has pointed out that "each sport contains a fundamental myth which it elaborates for its fans, and that our pleasure in watching such games derives in part from belonging briefly to the mythical world which the game and its players bring to life."[25] The spectator's involvement and fascination with sport, which he rarely receives in the workaday world, are dependent upon a shared tradition and shared fantasies. In the simplest terms, sport creates a larger, although more temporary, community than any other form of play in the modern world. The spectator's fascination with a mythic world apart from the dreary reality of his work is pointed up over and over again in sports fiction. Baseball is probably the most fertile source of mythic comparisons because it has the oldest and most available folk heritage of any major American sport. Books like *The Natural*, *The Great American Novel*, and *The Universal Baseball Association* would not be possible if a mythic superstructure were not already a part of the American consciousness. For example, because there was a Babe Ruth it is possible to make mythic-epic comparisons in *The Natural* between Ruth and Roy Hobbs. And because the intricate record-keeping tradition of baseball is almost one hundred years old, baseball becomes a marvelous metaphor for order and history in *The Universal Baseball Association*. The sense of a dynamic, developing tradition reinforces the ritual and mythic nature of sports.

Sport touches so many aspects of American life that it is an essential part of the American ethos. Robert H. Boyle has summed up the impact of sport this way: "Sport permeates any number of levels of contemporary society, and it touches upon and deeply influences such disparate elements as status, race relations, business life, automotive design, clothing styles, the concept of the hero, language, and ethical values. For better or worse it gives form and substance to much in American life."[26] That form and substance, having become the subject matter of a number of exciting recent American novels, demands critical attention. The metaphors of sport are becoming increasingly literal interpretations of contemporary life; and that is why it is so important that sports fiction treats play as reality and suggests that an unplayful world is in fact unreal. It no longer seems appropriate to say that play and sport are like "life"; play and sport *are* life—or should be, if sport were always play. The play-attitude is as serious and real as any other existential phenomenon. The more fully that attitude may be internalized, the more suitable it will be as a survival strategy in a world turned grim and dead.

CHAPTER TWO

IRONIC DETERMINISM IN "FAT CITY"

Sport sociologists have often raised an important question: Can the spirit of play be saved when sport is organized, packaged, and commercialized for public consumption? That question is central to much recent sports fiction, especially novels of visceral realism like *North Dallas Forty* in which the play-attitude is subverted by ruthless business ethics and the overwhelming influence of computer technology. In Leonard Gardner's *Fat City*, however, the stark naturalism of the author's vision emphasizes that it is not so much professionalism as the weight of environment which prevents even the possibility of play. Most play theorists identify true play with human joy and freedom. Eugen Fink, for one, defines play as "an eminent manifestation of human freedom."[1] Fink goes on to describe how, when the play-attitude is present, human creativity is the natural concomitant to joy and freedom. A similar view is expressed by the psychologist Robert E. Neale, who defines full, mature play as an "adventure."[2] Such values as joy, freedom, and creativity are out of the question in *Fat City*. In Gardner's novel there is no one who "enjoys an almost limitless creativity," who "experiences himself as the lord of the products of his imagination."[3]

Like the protagonists of many earlier naturalist fictions, Billy Tully and Ernie Munger, two small-time boxers from Stockton, California, have very little imagination, indeed, and correspondingly little access to the world of play, or playful sport. Still, they want and need to feel that life may be made more tolerable, more controllable. With their manager, Ruben Luna, they seek to break the ugly confinement and desperation of their lives through boxing. They want to hit the jackpot, the American dream of independence, comfort, and fullness. But play and the search for what Wallace Stegner called "The Big Rock Candy Mountain" are present in *Fat City* only as grim illusions; and boxing becomes the means of a continuous, ungratified search for freedom and renewal. *Fat City* is a novel filled with naturalistic details and ironic juxtapositions, highly reminiscent of the work of Crane, Norris, and London. It describes an overwhelmingly literal place where the crushing burden of environment annihilates any true sense of individuality or freedom. Sadly, it is the vague and fruitless search for individuality, for the transforming qualities of play, that consumes Ernie Munger and Billy Tully in a cycle of despair completely beyond their control.

Gardner wastes no time in introducing the deadening realities of "Fat City." As the novel opens, Billy Tully, whose first and last names are similarly nondescript, peers out the window of his room in a cheap Stockton hotel and sees "a view of business buildings, church spires, chimneys, water towers, gas tanks and the low roofs of residences rising among leafless trees between absolutely flat streets. Along the sidewalk under his window, men passed between bars and liquor stores, cafes, secondhand stores and walk-up hotels. Pigeons the color of the street pecked in the gutters. . . . His shade was tattered, his light bulb dim, and his neighbors all seemed to have lung trouble" (pp. 3-4).[4] The powerful rush of details defines Stockton, California, Gardner's "Fat City," but we have all been there, to joyless and loveless places where desperation is no longer quiet and escape seems impossible. If Stockton has an upper class, a theater district, a college campus, or an art museum, we never see them. Gardner's vision is relentless: working class bars; flea-bag hotel rooms equipped with *True Confession* magazines; and farm worker buses stinking of cheap wine, human sweat, and urine. For Billy Tully, Ernie Munger, and Ruben Luna there is really no way out of Fat City. The oppression there is as real and as inescapable as Crane's Bowery was for Maggie.

The fate of Gardner's small-time boxers is as inevitable and impersonal as the course of the seasons. The would-be players in this novel always act out of the need to resolve some inner conflict, and so such "play" as boxing seems to provide is absolutely compulsive and may be more closely identified with work than with a creative, free adventure. The implications for *Fat City* of Neale's psychological definition of play are striking. He makes distinctions which elaborate the sad distance between the genuine play which results from harmony and the empty rituals which Tully and Munger act out. Neale argues that there are always elements of uncertainty and risk in play and that these elements comprise the adventure of the play experience.[5] The "player" who acts out of conflict, as Ernie Munger and Billy Tully always do, seeks to control his experience and transform it to his advantage. Recent sports fiction is filled with characters who refuse to accept the potential adventure of the play experience, and, instead, approach the play-sphere as extreme pragmatists. Indeed, Tully and Munger come back to boxing, again and again, out of the desperation caused by other, more degrading, work, and under the illusion that boxing is a means of escaping the reductive world of *Fat City*. Because they always act out of conflict rather than harmony, Tully and Munger must see the risks of boxing as similar to the uncertainties of any work experience. As Neale puts it:

The attitude of adventure includes caprice as well as control. In the world of work, risk is forced onto and feared by the individual, whereas in play, risk is freely accepted and even freely sought. The player does not choose his destiny . . . but follows a destiny which is revealed to him during the course of his adventure. It is for this reason that play is feared by the worker who is truly the one who seeks mastery of destiny, and it is for this reason that the player does not complain of bad luck.[6]

Billy Tully and Ernie Munger always complain about their bad luck. Their strivings are so vain that they seek to use boxing not as free play, not as a creative adventure, but as an escape from tedium and degradation. The appeal of boxing is psychological; it is the instrument through which the would-be player attempts to control and change his life. That very control which Tully and Munger seek, as they try to actualize their desires through boxing, becomes a mere parody of play. Boxing is thus a source of worklike mastery and has nothing in common with the play-attitude or with the potential adventure of play. Indeed, boxing is the instrument of a horrible irony in *Fat City*. When life seems most intolerable, Ernie, Billy, and Ruben look to boxing for some freedom or escape from other, more menial work. Because boxing is at least a source of male pride and camaraderie in *Fat City*, it is work which can be identified with. But while boxing may seem to promise escape, while things may even seem temporarily to get better, ultimate escape is impossible, and the freedom gained is utterly illusory. Boxing, by engaging its participants in a constantly frustrated quest, becomes the instrument of *Fat City's* ironic determinism.

Boxing, like most sports, is a territorial game. Two men are bound to defend the same ring, a small and intimate place in which they punish each other physically at the same time that they must clinch each other's bodies, smell each other's sweat, and anticipate each other's strategy. Boxing is also typical of most sports in that the individual participant's performance must be translated through judges and a referee. There are situations, such as fouls, technical knockouts, or close decisions, in which the judgment of the referee is crucial. Still, boxing is a highly individual sport. What a participant does physically and strategically directly affects his success or failure in the ring. Unlike baseball, where a perfect double-play ball may take a bad hop, or football, where a perfect touchdown pass may be dropped, in boxing there are (or should be) almost no intermediaries to militate against the individual's performance. In sports, unlike most of contemporary life, one's opponents are usually clear, especially when the play-attitude is preserved. And since "sports are one of the last outposts where physical aggression has an established acceptable place in our culture,"[7] boxing would seem to be an appropriate metaphor for the individual's struggle in a totally impersonal and degrading environment. But in *Fat City* the fighter is stripped of even the dignity of his performance in the ring. There are fixes and petty commercial influences here which mock the individual's effort to locate a single, defeatable foe. In playful sport the body is not an instrument; one becomes one's body.[8] However, in *Fat City* the body becomes a dull machine, which only serves as a means to another end, an end which itself does not exist. The emphasis here is on mindless brawn, the body degraded and destroyed for temporary, finally meaningless, victories. The "one on one" metaphor of boxing is completely ironic in Gardner's novel, for in *Fat City* victory in the ring, like any other kind of escape, and at whatever price, is completely illusory, and thus "Fat City" becomes an image, not of fullness and comfort, but of the anguish of men who try to assert their freedom and individuality, but who never succeed, who never can succeed.

In his study of the black fighter, Nathan Hare has pointed out that "fighters are the products of the racial hostilities and socioeconomic conflicts in which they live."[9] They generally come from the most oppressed ethnic and racial groups in urban areas, and thus Irish, Jewish, and then Italian fighters dominated boxing in the first half of this century. Since then black and Spanish-American fighters have predominated.[10] But the denial of the play-attitude is reductive in *Fat City* and levels many of these ethnic and racial differences. Tully's sham racial values are small compensation when one lives, as he does, in cheap hotels where winos and bums are always hacking and coughing and "smudges from oily heads darkened the wallpaper between the metal rods of his bed" (p. 3).

In *Fat City* boxing is a source of masculine identity. Sexual identity and self-respect become one for Ernie, Billy, and Ruben. Women are important adornments to male identity, but they have no independent identity of their own. The simple-minded identification of masculinity with fighting is the source of a good deal of ironic tension in the novel, even to the point where the male ego is actively hostile toward women. For example, earlier in Tully's career, when he began to lose against first-class competition, what he needed most from his wife, but never received, was some "recognition of the rites of virility" (p. 12). Tully had used his wife as an ornament when he was winning, when he was a local hero, and she, correspondingly, was no longer interested in him when he began to lose. By not recognizing "the rites of virility," Tully's wife participated in the denial of his masculine identity brought on by defeat. And "masculine" identity, which is no identity at all, was all that he had.

For Ernie Munger boxing has a similar meaning. After his first sparring session at the Lido Gym, Ernie banters with another newcomer in the shower. They talk about typical locker room subjects, but when Ernie finishes dressing we realize that he has experienced one of the book's more liberating moments: "Drawing on his pants, Ernie, bruised, fatigued and elated, felt he had joined the company of men" (p. 17). Of course, he has not, even if such company actually exists in some remote realm. Gardner's ironic deflation here is the first of many such passages which point up how pervasive Ernie's illusion is.

Before Ernie's first amateur fight, he is preoccupied with seducing his girl friend, Faye. Love and satisfaction are out of the question here. Sexual experience in the form of an objective conquest—only intercourse will do—is a prerequisite for the more important intercourse that takes place between two men in a ring: "To appear in the ring tomorrow without ever having won this other battle seemed presumptuous and dangerous. He alone in the Lido Gym carried a burden of silence and deceptive innuendo, and he wondered if this could mean the difference between victory and defeat" (p. 33). The next evening Ernie boasts in the locker room to Buford Wills that he was "out getting a little last night." Ironically, the acknowledgement of fourteen-year-old Buford is the final sanction of Ernie's sexual exploits. Ernie has indeed lost his virginity, but after the act of "ecstatic oblivion," having "realized he had experienced the ultimate in pleasure," Ernie must turn to Faye and ask, "Was it good?" (p. 34).

If this sounds like the old chauvinist slop, it is because the debasement of women, treating them as adornments, conquests, and possessions, is an especially important part of the dehumanizing world of *Fat City*. This relentless narrowing is nowhere more pointedly seen than after Tully's comeback victory over Arcadio Lucero. Tully has moved out of Oma's apartment without even taking his clothes. He moves out because she is ruining his training habits with her constant boozing and self-pitying depression. Her flabby body has never really excited him, but rather intensified the loss of his wife. Living with Oma is a painfully acute symptom for Tully of how totally lost he really is. And yet, "after having beaten Lucero he deserved a woman. . . . He was walking not in the direction of his hotel but toward Oma's, feeling capable of knocking on her door, of saying he had come only for his clothes, of putting them in his suitcase and then methodically stripping her, taking her without the slightest intrusion on his isolate self, then picking up his suitcase and leaving forever" (p. 153). Tully's true reward for his victory over Lucero is a momentary glimpse of what he considers his masculine identity. To know who you are, and, better still, to have others know who you are, is the real prize of fighting. Unfortunately, Tully's definition of masculinity is necessarily so limited that boxing can never tell him who he is, yet he labors under the illusion that it does.

Surely the most horrifying emotion in the passage above is the intense hostility that Tully obviously feels toward women. When Tully arrives at Oma's, Earl unexpectedly answers the door and indicates that he has moved back in with Oma, that Tully's bag has been packed and is ready to be taken. But what is really interesting in the scene is that while Oma is cursing at Tully, showing the ugliest, most profane side of her personality, Earl talks with Tully about the fight with Lucero, congratulates him, and indicates that he might catch one of his future fights. Oma is irrelevant to the camaraderie of two men who are almost strangers to each other; she is the common property that each *uses*, but what they really *share* is boxing. The scene echoes an earlier one in which Earl, Oma, and Tully were talking and drinking in the Harbor Inn. Oma was excoriating Earl instead of Tully, but again it was the men who seemed to be getting on. Earl bought Tully a drink and they talked, inevitably, about fighting. In *Fat City* the moments of deepest and keenest undering are always between men, but that understanding rests on empty fantasy and not only excludes women, but may be openly hostile to them. The sham masculine values of *Fat City* are thus ultimately as sterile as the place itself.

Tully's "isolate self" is typical of all the men in the novel. Those moments between men and women which we are prepared to accept as most loving and tender are always perverted, made impersonal, often meaningless. Ruben makes love to his wife "silently addressing her with a name not her own" and persevering to "a realm beyond all personality" (p. 22). And Ernie, filled with panic upon hearing that Faye wants "to be good for [him]," "to cook for [him]," kisses her "lax waiting mouth with exquisite unhappiness" (p. 81). Love in *Fat City* is the mindless drift of bodies coming together out of a sense of duty rather than inclination, or, as Ernie so poignantly says, "I'd want somebody so it'd seem worth getting my ass kicked . . . so I could . . . I don't know . . . have a home." (The ellipses here are Gardner's, p. 81.)

And he really does not know. Although his attitude is puerile, how could Ernie have any higher understanding of love? His family life is as depressing as his job on the late-night shift as gas station attendant. He seldom sees his father, and his "association" with his mother has for a long time been merely "perfunctory." The sterility of Ernie's life is defined by a catalog of dreary details, a summary of the wasted landscape he passes while running to keep in shape: "he ran along the dirt road past burnt mattresses, water heaters, fenders, sodden cartons, worn-out tires and rusty cans strewn down the steep bank. At the shore rocked bottles and driftwood, blackened tules, and occasionally a reeking, belly-up fish" (p. 26). Running is Ernie's way of metaphorically outdistancing his environment. Gardner marvellously captures the hopelessness of this kind of existence in one of the book's very few overtly symbolic passages: "Gagging on a dry throat, he chose some object as his finish line and, plodding up to it on weighted legs, plodded right on past. . . . he strained on to a farther landmark. He did not quit there either. He fought on with himself. . . . until at last he stood gasping on the muddy bank of the point with nowhere else to run" (pp. 26-27).

Although we realize intuitively that Ernie will never really make it as a fighter, fighting is the one aspect of his life that he feels hopeful about. Typically, it is the one part of Ernie's personality that Faye cannot understand, because being a fighter is part of Ernie's sexual identity. For example, one afternoon Ernie has an argument with a driver who has cut in front of him. Faye is worried that a fight will ensue, and Ernie, in turn, is miffed that his wife apparently does not respect his fighting prowess. He wonders, "who does she think she married? And it seemed that she neither knew nor respected him, that she denied the very basis of his personality" (p. 89). And the reason for this gap in Faye's understanding is entirely sexual—"She was a girl, after all, and could have no sure sense of who he was" (p. 89).

Marriage does nothing to change Ernie's understanding of women, nor does it in any significant way alter the quality of his life. He changes the dreariness of his parents' house for "three rooms on the ground floor of an old, three-story, white shingle apartment house. The kitchen faced onto garbage cans and lawn chairs in a back yard enclosed by a hedge, and dishes occasionally vibrated in the cabinet from a motor idling beyond the wall" (p. 88). Marriage also ensures that Ernie's boxing career will never amount to much. The hopefulness he feels about coming back into training is always balanced (as with Tully) by long periods of inactivity. The responsibilities of a wife and child make success as a fighter impossible, not because a boxing career cannot be successful, but because Ernie always approaches training as a means to a quick buck. He cannot afford to approach boxing playfully, only manipulatively, and so whatever play boxing may be susceptible to is never realized. The failure to grasp the potential adventure here means not only that Ernie's boxing will not be playful, but also that his encounters with the sport will be sporadic, only minimally successful, and thus ultimately futile as a means of escape, renewal, or fulfillment.

Perhaps we may excuse Ernie his hypocrisy and immaturity since he is, after all, only eighteen. But in *Fat City* there are no signs that love and understanding deepen with age. Tully on the verge of his thirtieth birthday is more crudely juvenile than Ernie. He lives with Oma for awhile not because he loves or desires her, but because even living with a neurotically depressed alcoholic is better than being alone. And if Ernie and Faye should stay together for twenty years or more, we can see a forecast of their marriage in Ruben Luna's impatience at having to go trick-or-treating with his children and his dismay over his wife's corpulence.

The key tension in *Fat City* is between the confinement, anguish, and degeneracy of Stockton and the futile quest for freedom and renewal always associated with boxing. Stockton is a physical wasteland as well as an emotional one. Image by image, Gardner presents us with a world of total squalor. In *Fat City* El Dorado Street is not lined with gold, but rather with ranks of "leaners drinking from cans and pint bottles discreetly covered by paper bags" (p. 59). The tedium and meanness of Stockton's poor are summed up in the following passage:

They talked, watched, drifted in and out of crowded bars and cardrooms, cafes, poolhalls, liquor stores and movies, their paths crossed by lines of urine from darkened doorways. Around the area cruised squadcars and patrol wagons with their pairs of peering faces. The fallen, the reeling and violent were conveyed away. Ambulances came driven by policemen. Fire trucks arrived and sodden, smoking mattresses were dragged out to the pavement. Evangelists came with small brass bands. Sometimes a corpse was taken down from a hotel. Occasionally in *The Stockton Record* there was an editorial deploring blight. [P. 85]

Even the natural environment of the city is not free of the sweeping blight. In Washington Square one finds "scores of men, prone, supine, sitting, some wearing coats in the June heat, their wasted bodies motionless on the grass" (p. 59). Tree surgeons come to the square and methodically cut down all the shade trees. The dispossessed sojourners of the park assume the trees must have been diseased. We never learn for sure, but the explanation seems both reasonable and appropriate because Gardner's "Fat City," like Eliot's "Wasteland," is "a heap of broken images, where the sun beats, and the dead tree gives no shelter. . . ."

Surrounding Stockton are the fertile fields of the San Joaquin River delta. The fertility of the fields is ironically juxtaposed against the brutally degrading work of day laborers topping onions, thinning tomatoes, or sacking walnuts. These jobs are usually relegated to blacks, Mexicans, and Filipinos, and yet, at first, Tully sanctimoniously takes consolation in the fact that he is white and a boxer. He soon discovers, however, that being an athlete is poor preparation for the backbreaking work of thinning tomatoes. Tully is just another member of a "brief tableaux of upright wincing men, hoes dangling, their hands on the small of their backs, who were going on under the same torment—some of them winos, donut and coffee men, chain smokers, white-bread eaters, maybe none ever athletes yet all moving steadily on while he fell farther and farther behind . . ." (p. 74). Tully tries as long as he can to console himself with his whiteness, but as he feels his will receding, as the smells of liniment and urine become more prevalent, the attempt collapses. His desperation obliterates any smug superiority he might have felt.

Ernie's job at the gas station is hardly more interesting; his major responsibility is to keep the toilet locked. Eventually, the responsibilities of marriage bring him to the fields where he sacks walnuts for some extra money and meets Tully for the second time. Tully, with typical bravado, gets Ernie on his sacking crew, but his triumph is short-lived. Farm work is degrading; he does not want to appear too familiar with it, and so the talk inevitably turns to boxing: "Afraid he might appear to be nothing but a farm worker, he began to talk about getting back into shape, finding encouragement in the fact that Ernie, after that disappointing day in the YMCA, had actually become a boxer" (p. 117).

In the above passage one hears the echo of a phrase which haunts the entire novel: "getting back into shape." No phrase better epitomizes the illusory freedom and empty quest that boxing represents in *Fat City*. Getting back into shape is the road to fighting, and fighting is the hoped-for escape from menial farm work, from suffocating women like Oma, from total degradation. But Tully's momentary victory in the ring, one which his body pays dearly for, makes his ultimate defeat all the more devastating.

Talking to Ernie in the fields, Tully, animated by the companionship of a fellow boxer, someone capable of understanding his ambitions and frustrations, becomes increasingly expansive and optimistic about returning to the game: "I'm just a damn fool wasting my time out here. . . . But you get in a bind. . . . I got my responsibilities too. . . . I got a woman on my hands and that means getting up at four and breaking your back all day. But if I can start fighting again that'll be the end of that. . . . All I need's a fight and a woman. Then I'm set. I get the fight I'll get the woman" (p. 119). Boxing always gives rise to the grim illusion that things are going to get better. Tully's logic for success is as inevitable as the certainty of his ultimate failure. Tully is incapable of approaching boxing, the potential adventure, on its own terms. He insists, as everyone else in *Fat City* insists, that he can manipulate the play experience and turn it to his advantage. Ironically, so long as he does this the "play" experience will always be motivated by Tully's intense desire to resolve his own conflicts—despair over farm labor, his living conditions, the loss of his wife, and his life with Oma—and can never be more than a worklike experience. This central irony is mirrored in Ernie's experience as well, for he returns to boxing for exactly the same reason that he shows up at the farm worker buses. Like Ernie and Ruben, Tully sees the game in only the crudest, most inartistic terms. His "play" is always grounded in the sordid, literal reality of *Fat City* and is never personalized or transformed in any way to make it more susceptible to an adventure.

Significantly, Tully makes his optimistic remarks about fighting after he and Oma have spent an evening talking with Esteban Escobar. Tully has been seeing posters around the town announcing Escobar's next fight, and while he and Escobar had been at their peaks at the same time, it depresses Tully that Escobar is still fighting. Piqued, and jealous of Escobar's durability, Tully recounts his fight with Fermin Soto, which he now regards as the turning point in his career. According to Tully, he was beating Soto badly when gushing cuts over each of his (Tully's) eyes forced the referee to stop the fight. The cuts were caused by razor blades illegally hidden in Soto's gloves, and had Ruben been with Tully he would have protested the fight immediately. But Tully was alone, his cornermen were probably in on the fix, and by the time Ruben saw the cuts back in Stockton it was too late to file a complaint. Escobar is mildly interested in the story and offers his glib commiseration, but he is much more interested in his platinum blond girl friend, and soon Tully is talking to himself: "I been thinking about giving it one last try. . . . I just let myself go all to pot. I'm going to start doing some running. If I can get in shape I know I can still fight" (p. 113).

So the litany goes. In *Fat City* men talk about boxing, about getting back in shape, when they feel most confined. Ruben runs down the latest developments at the Lido Gym each evening for his wife, not because she is really interested in Buford Wills or Ernie Munger, but because his compulsive chatter is a momentary stay against the confinement of home and family. The gym, like the Harbor Inn or the Azores Hotel, is ironically named for the illusory escape it represents for the denizens of *Fat City*. The Azores Hotel is run by "an old man with broken capillaries" who leads Tully to "a cold narrow room" with "large stains the color of tobacco juice" on the "rippled wallpaper" (p. 162). And the Harbor Inn, a fitting refuge for Stockton's down-and-outs, carries the following elegant notice:

> PLEASE DON'T SPIT
> ON THE FLOOR
> GET UP AND SPIT
> IN THE TOILET BOWL
> I thank you. [P. 7]

Everything in *Fat City* is deflated by the vivid flow of naturalistic details which defines it. The one overwhelming presence in this novel is the confinement of the city itself, a squalor so pervasive that no one and nothing can escape it.

When that confinement is most intolerable, Tully seeks literally to break it: "He fought urges to hurl his tumbler out the window. The chair he sat on smashed in his mind against the wall. Yearning for struggle and release, he felt he had to fight, as he had felt years before when he had come home from the army to begin his life and confronted the fact that there was nothing he wanted to do" (p. 109). Not only is there nothing Tully wants to do, but there is also nothing he is really qualified to do except engage in the dreary illusion symbolized by fighting. Tully's total desperation on the day he meets Ernie in the fields is mirrored in the absolute repugnance he felt for Oma the night before: "In bed beside her he lay motionless, repelled by the thought of contacting her with even a toe. . . . As he inched up an arm, straightened a leg, his muscles seemed to pulse on their bones in an agony of confinement. He was balked. His life seemed near its end. In four days he would be thirty" (pp. 114-115). Thus, the optimism of Tully's conversation with Ernie the next day takes on even more importance. Because Tully sees boxing as the only escape from sordid routine, he *must* come back to it out of desperation. And since his hope is illusory, his desperation ensures that his ultimate failure will be all the more devastating.

That is indeed what happens. Ernie and Tully do show up at the Lido Gym, to try one more time to get back in shape. For Tully, this training period before the fight with Arcadio Lucero is the only time he seems capable of coping with Oma. He is even strong enough to move out of her apartment—with help from Ruben—when he realizes that she is ruining his training habits. The fight itself typifies the hopelessness of Tully's struggle. His opponent is Arcadio Lucero, a tired, journeyman fighter, who, essentially, is Tully's Mexican double. Both men are twenty-nine, past their primes physically, in debt to their managers, and fighting to escape the humiliation of other work. Earlier in their careers both men enjoyed modest popularity; the "moments of limitless destiny" Lucero felt among his young admirers are reminiscent of Tully's ecstasy entering the Stockton auditorium arm in arm with his wife, Lynn. Tully is thus really fighting himself. And although he lasts the full ten rounds and wins a tough decision, the victory is finally empty. He comes away with a mere $100; in a local bar the beerchasers are interested in the drinks he is buying, not in his victory; and at Oma's apartment he finds that Earl has moved back in. The entire evening has left him more doomed than prior to his return to the gym: "Before he had reached his hotel a ghastly depression came over him, a buzzing wave of confusion and despair, and he knew absolutely that he was lost" (p. 156). Boxing thus elaborates the futile quest for freedom. Without boxing, life for Tully would be consistent squalor; with it, his despair is a rhythmic cycle which, because it is so frustrating, always plunges him more deeply into the degradation of *Fat City*.

Beyond the empty fellowship of men there is only the impersonal force of fate. Survival in *Fat City* is determined by impersonal forces; escape is a mirage. Tully never trusts or believes in anyone, least of all himself, and so his life is a cycle of ungratified hope and weighty despair. Ruben, who has known the worst times in boxing and come through them, has a "fatalistic optimism . . . and though he was not immune to anxiety over his boxers, he felt he was immune to despair. . . . He knew he could last" (p. 162). And Ernie, the book's most naive protagonist, still has the resiliency of youth. He returns from Salt Lake City "feeling in himself the potent allegiance of fate," an optimism which we know is completely unwarranted (p. 183).

Yet an allegiance to fate seems the most appropriate image for the final passage of a novel so insistent on repetitious cycles which bring only more of the same. The novel ends in spring. But spring in *Fat City* does not herald rebirth and rejuvenation. It is still another ironic symbol of unchanging misery, as if the seasons, like the lush San Joaquin delta, mock the sterility of Stockton. Tully, we learn from one of Ruben's fighters, is working as a cook, the same kind of job he held when we first met him. Inevitably, "he had talked about getting into shape" (p. 169). In Stockton the pattern of life remains unchanged: "The rains ceased; new green leaves covered the elms and sycamores lining residential streets. . . . As summer approached, hundreds of men were again on El Dorado Street, leaning against storefronts, cars and parking meters" (p. 169). Ernie is about to go to Salt Lake City to fight a preliminary bout. Ortega, Ruben's current heavyweight, has come down with the flu and so there is no longer traveling money for Ruben. Are we supposed to remember Tully's fight with Fermin Soto, when he also traveled alone because there was no expense money for Ruben? Ernie is not victimized in the ring as Tully was, but his total naiveté with the two girls who strand him in the desert indicates that whatever small victories he does win are gratuitous.

And for Ruben someone will always be in training. Someone will always want to fight, for boxing, like everything else in *Fat City*, conforms to the monotonous, inescapable cycle of a seasonal progression leading never to spring but to winter and death. He's looking for the one-in-a-million fighter who will carry him out of Fat City altogether, but his petty commercialism ensures that his fighters will never make it. When Ruben calls Owen Mackin to arrange a comeback fight for Tully, he thinks Tully might be overmatched by Lucero. But he accepts the match anyway because any fight is better than none at all. Tully suspects that Ruben has succumbed to pressure, and he is right. After Ernie wins his comeback fight Ruben's praise is grossly overzealous. Ernie is suddenly "the most colorful lightweight in Northern California" (p. 147). And when Ernie fights in Salt Lake City, Ruben bills him as "Irish Ernie Munger" so the local fans will know he is white and show up to root for him. Ernie hasn't a bit of Irish ancestry, but the gate is more important to Ruben than a small public relations lie. Whatever good intentions Ruben has toward his fighters are always undercut by his pettiness. He is always willing to feed Tully or lend him a few dollars, but only in the hope of luring him back into training.

Thus Ruben, a relatively sympathetic character, unwittingly reinforces the ironic determinism that boxing represents. He may entice Tully back into training, but only to renew the frustrating quest for escape and continue the cycle of despair. And so Ruben goes on, the pattern of his life determined by the equally determined fortunes of men like Ernie Munger and Billy Tully. When Tully fails to show up again after Ruben lends him fifteen dollars, he accepts his loss calmly, resigned to the disappointment fighters have been causing him for years, knowing that "when Tully wanted to fight again . . . he would come back to the gym" (p. 169).

CHAPTER THREE

"NORTH DALLAS FORTY"

Professionalism and the Corruption of Play

Sport always reflects, with poignant accuracy, the culture from which it comes. It becomes, in Howard Slusher's words, a "declaration of the culture." Slusher goes on to contrast American sport and its "technological and materialistic values" with the more philosophical emphasis of Eastern sport. He compares the deeply philosophical and transcendent nature of archery, as it is revealed in Herrigel's *Zen in the Art of Archery*, with the American version of fencing, which relies on electrical gadgetry to make accurate judgments.[1] Slusher's comparison is a good one because fencing is a sport which we tend to associate with grace and beauty; it is a sport much older than the industrial revolution. Even in such an ancient sport (Huizinga reminds us that the duel was originally a play form) the contemporary demand for "accuracy" has, in the West at least, changed the nature of the game. While one might expect any American sport to have at least some technological biases, football is the technological sport *par excellence*. As such, it emphasizes many of the values of contemporary America.

Murray Ross has pointed out that the essential myth of football is a heroic one.[2] Football players dress like warriors, with much protective padding and helmets which mask their faces. Football is also a game of staggering complexity; it is impossible for the individual spectator to take in each of the movements of twenty-two players which comprise a single play. Most players' identities are reduced to their numerals, with only the exceptional backs and receivers able to display their special idiosyncrasies. It is a rare *aficionado* indeed who can recognize the "style" of a pulling guard or a defensive tackle. Football is a modern game which emphasizes extreme specialization and computer technology. And while there are still a few scrambling quarterbacks and "free-lance" defensive specialists, football emphasizes the cohesion of a "perfectly coordinated unit," and with machinelike precision smothers most individual personality. Moreover, the players themselves cannot afford to consider the "feelings" of their competitors. John McMurtry, a former professional football player, has pointed out that "the truly professional attitude is simply not to think of him [the opponent] as a human being at all—he is a 'position' to be removed as efficiently as possible in order to benefit the team's corporate enterprise of gaining points. The mask over his face and all the covering equipment reinforce his status of non-humanity."[3]

McMurtry goes on to itemize the key values of both football and the so-called "reality" outside the game: "exclusive possession, acquisitiveness, relentless violence, impersonality, ruthless competition, technological sophistication and strict authoritarianism."[4] In Peter Gent's *North Dallas Forty* it becomes clear that the world of professional football is at the center of American capitalism, and that, more than a metaphor for American values, professional football is a microcosm of contemporary social problems. Unlike *Fat City*, where petty commercialism is subordinate to the despair of the frustrated quest, the emphasis in *North Dallas Forty* is on the ways play and sport may be perverted when commercialized. The extreme violence and conformity of professional football clearly violate the joy, freedom, and creativity of the play-attitude. But there is also a more subtle perversion of play in *North Dallas Forty*. In sport the play-attitude is a direct, often visceral, involvement; it is a physical, as well as emotional and psychological, experience. Professional sport has changed the emphasis of the potential play experience from the activity of the player himself to the indirect, reflective experience of the spectator. Thus play in *North Dallas Forty* is undermined not only by excessive violence, rigid conformity, and an overriding technology, but also by the triumph of vicarious over direct experience.

A great many play theorists denounce professional sport as a perversion of the play impulse. Huizinga's definition of play includes the restriction that "it is an activity connected with no material interest, and no profit can be gained by it."[5] Paul Weiss, in his philosophy of sport, agrees with Huizinga; play, he says, is nonproductive, and cannot produce economically viable goods.[6] And the psychologist Erik Erikson argues that play "does not produce commodities. Where it does, it 'goes professional.' "[7] Each of these men, writing from very different perspectives, has seen that the "selling" of play is a threat to its autonomy. While the threat to the player's freedom and creativity in professional sport is a real one, it is important to understand that this opinion has been unduly strengthened by the implicit belief of each of these writers that play and work are opposites. Erikson goes so far as to say that "even the most strenuous and dangerous play is by definition not work."[8]

As has been pointed out in the introductory remarks, such dualisms as play/work and play/reality are naive. They fail to take account of the increasingly obscure relationship between work and its products in a technologically sophisticated age. It is true that professional sport rarely epitomizes the joy, creativity, and freedom which Huizinga, Fink, and others associate with play. However, the examples of figures like Babe Ruth, Dizzy Dean, Fran Tarkenton, and Willie Mays, and more recently, Mark Fidrych, make it clear that professional sport may be playful, creative, free, even anarchic. Rather than dichotomizing and saying that professional sport is either work because it is productive or play because it is a game, it may be more helpful to talk about the specific ways in which play may or may not be perverted when it becomes productive.

In *Fat City* commercialism in sport is merely a small detail, a petty insult to the play-attitude, which is impossible even in potential in that grisly world. The cyclical rhythm of life in *Fat City* reinforces the inevitability of despair and failure there. The high-powered catalogs of details ensure that we understand the desperation of *Fat City*, a desperation which is absolutely antagonistic to the liberation of play. But professional sport is the very substance of *North Dallas Forty*. And although both books are about individual survival, the possibility of achieving that survival through play has been preempted in *Fat City*. The world of *North Dallas Forty* is strikingly different from *Fat City*. The realistic details here are of the richest, most powerful, and, for some of us, the most glamorous people in American sport. In *North Dallas Forty* play *is* possible, and so, manifested as football or love, it is at least a potential means for surviving an impersonal environment of violence, racism, and conformity.

North Dallas Forty is the story of eight days in the life of Phil Elliott, flanker for the National Football League's Dallas team. As the narrator of his own story, Phil carefully elucidates the madness and hypocrisy of professional football and the society which has made it the most popular and lucrative sport in America. The ambiguous nature of professional football is highlighted by the irony of our impulse to talk about the game as play in the face of the overwhelming evidence that it is a brutally competitive business. For the player there is a Catch-22 quality about this paradox. O. W. Meadows, in his most eloquent moment, captures the players' ambivalence during an argument with assistant coach Johnson: "You never give us anything to take into a game but fucking facts. I'm sick of goddam tendencies. It's a goddam business for you but it's s'pose' to be a sport to us" (p. 275).[9] Of course, Johnson replies that Meadows should not worry about the spirit of play, teamwork, or camaraderie. He is supposed to be a "professional."

The heavy emphasis of Phil's narrative is so critical of the elements of the sport antagonistic to the play-attitude (or any form of liberation, creativity, or nonconformity for that matter) that an appropriate preliminary question might well be: Why engage in sports at all? In a world so dehumanized why not sell insurance or real estate, or work for Texas Instruments? There is no ambiguity about work and play in those jobs; when we sell insurance we know damn well that we are working. The point is that for all the violence, impersonality, and machinelike precision of professional football, for all the arduous practices, computerized game strategies, and interminable therapy sessions, football, the game itself, may be a totally compelling form of play.[10] " 'Job! Job!' Meadows screamed into Johnson's face. 'I don't want no fucking job, I wanna play football' " (p. 275).

Aside from the time he spends with Charlotte Caulder, the only moments of real freedom and joy that Phil experiences are those when he is playing flanker. Even in practice, the thrill of catching a football temporarily transports him beyond his precarious status with the team. For example, there is this description from Tuesday's practice: "Four more steps and I would be to the middle linebacker. I looked back for the ball. Maxwell had already released it. It thumped into my chest, a full step before I reached the middle linebacker, his hand waving uselessly in the air. Goddam, I loved to catch a football" (p. 63). And on Thursday, when Maxwell informs Phil that B.A. is going to use him more in Sunday's game, the effect on Phil is immediate. Although he realizes that he is an "optional accessory" to B.A.'s "winning machine," Phil cannot deny the exhilaration of playing. Once involved in the flow of the game the true player is intent upon performance. Winning and losing, means and ends are all secondary to the experience itself.

Other potentially liberating experiences, such as those provided by drugs and sex, cannot match the intensity of the play experience. As for drugs, Phil has taken everything from marijuana to amyl nitrite to cocaine; codeine and vitamin B12 are part of his regular diet. Drugs are closely tied to football in *North Dallas Forty*. Rather than heightening the player's experience, or inducing a new experience, drugs have a deadening effect. When provided by the club they deaden his pain; when taken surreptitiously by the player they deaden his fear. Yet in spite of the "fictions and personal contradictions" underlying his participation in professional football, "the thrill of playing was no less real and that thrill is indescribable. Doing something better than anyone else in front of millions of people. It is the highest I have ever been" (p. 178).

The feeling that emerges from these descriptions is ecstatic. Of course, we realize that the state Phil is describing is evanescent, yet there is something about his exhilaration which transcends purely logical description. As Howard Slusher has pointed out in his existential analysis of sport, sport does not free man *from* other activities such as work, but is itself freedom.[11] Or from an ontological perspective, Fink tells us that "Each game is an attempt at existence, a vital experiment that encounters in the plaything the essence of unyielding reality."[12] Ideally, one comes to understand more fully just who he or she is: "Each encounter provides a reason for being; but more than justification of existence sport provides its own rationale."[13] This is surely the initial attraction of sport for any player, the unconscious knowledge that, as Slusher puts it, "Sport is more than simply what one does in his leisure; it is more than an escape from everyday life; and certainly it is more than a mere socially desirable avenue for release of one's aggressions. The *understanding of being* is clarified by sport."[14]

Phil is acutely aware of the existential value of sport in his life. More than anything else football is a means of achieving, at least momentarily, a total awareness of the self and its potential. As Phil explains to Maxwell after Sunday's game, "there is a basic reality where it is just me and the job to be done, the game and all its skills. And the reward wasn't what other people thought or how much they paid me but how I felt at the moment I was exhibiting my special skill. How I felt about me. That's what's true. That's what I loved. All the rest is just a matter of opinion" (p. 285). What Phil is really talking about here is self-awareness and authenticity. No one in *Fat City* ever experiences anything like the self-awareness Phil shows in these passages. The deep inner conflict with which Ernie Munger and Billy Tully approach sport prevents it from ever being more than a desperate worklike experience. But Phil Elliott *is* able, for occasional moments, to approach sport playfully, to immerse himself in the flow of the game itself and not its products.

We must remember that Phil's explanation, which Maxwell accepts, is the *initial* reason for playing. When the game becomes commercialized and the instincts of offensive and defensive players are reduced to statistically effective game plans, the play impulse is perverted. Only momentary flashes of joy and freedom are still available to most professional football players. Self-awareness is much more likely to come in the disagreeable form of endless replays of one's mistakes during the weekly review of game films. While Phil still naively wants the game to be fun, Maxwell realizes that the initial play impulse must be subordinated to the business concerns of a professional. The sense and the essence of playing for Phil are not "winning or losing, but the means: the game. That's the reason— the game, only the game" (p. 286). The evidence of *North Dallas Forty* clearly shows such an attitude to be dangerously private, so far from reality as almost to be mad. We can see the cynical distance Maxwell has traveled as a professional in his rejoinder to Phil: "All I know is what I have to do statistically to keep playing and that's what I try to do each week. I enjoy playing, that's great, but I need those numbers first and have to do whatever is necessary to get 'em" (p. 286). Maxwell certainly has the instincts necessary for survival in the world of professional football. Or perhaps one should say he has an *understanding* of the business of professional football which helps him to survive. It is Phil's reaction which is *instinctive*. He wants to have fun playing football, a quality in keeping with the original nature of the game. Maxwell understands that in professional football fun is irrelevant to survival.

Maxwell's significance is that, by the standards of the Dallas management, he is normal, in touch with the reality of the game as a business, and thus he always points up Phil's naiveté. Play may be possible in this world, but far from being essential, it is a real hindrance to success and personal survival. The wiser Phil Elliott who narrates *North Dallas Forty* has learned "that survival is the reason of life and that fear and hatred are the emotions. What you cannot overcome by hatred you must fear" (p. 142). And so Phil fears everything from the military industrial complex to the management of the Dallas team. The emphasis of both organizations is upon strict authoritarianism and conformity, goals which are antagonistic to the spirit of play.

Whatever this fear may be, it permeates both professional football and the larger environment of contemporary America. In both contexts, pervasive fear and an emphasis on very limited, competitive values annihilates the play-attitude. By making the professional athlete uncertain about his status, management ensures that he will fear his work, and that his experience of football will be one of deep conflict and thus not play. Phil recognizes very early on that the camaraderie of sport is merely a fiction of professional football. The player is ultimately alone, isolated from his teammates by the artificially heightened competitive spirit. When Phil is benched after having been the team's starting flanker, he hopes that Billy Gill, his replacement, will do poorly. B. A., the Dallas coach, has replaced him with Gill because he wants to make Phil more "controllable." Gill is not nearly as effective a receiver, but, given the chance to start, B. A. knows he will be totally cooperative. And by reducing Phil to a bench-warmer B. A. hopes to make him more appreciative of his now-rare opportunities to play. Phil thus sees Gill as less of a threat to his position than B. A. and Clinton Foote, self-righteous men who seek to augment their personal success and power by exploiting others. And so there is little room for independent spirit and individuality on the team. No matter how talented and indispensable an individual player may be, he must be convinced of his own worthlessness to make him more controllable. "When an athlete, no matter what color jersey he wears, finally realizes that opponents and teammates alike are his adversaries . . . he is on his way to understanding the spirit that underlies the business of competitive sport. There is no team, no loyalty, no camaraderie; there is only him, alone" (p. 28).

The first major perversion of the play-attitude is thus a mechanical and conformist reductivism. *North Dallas Forty* portrays professional football as a completely dehumanized locale where the spirit of play has been corrupted by the spirit of the machine. Those players who actively rebel against the conformity imposed upon them, like Thomas Richardson or Phil Elliott, are destroyed by management. Only Seth Maxwell seems to have sufficient resiliency to survive, but he purchases that survival at the cost of his sensitivity. He has become an unthinking, graceless, insensitive boor. There is also strong evidence that he may be a trickster, an informer. Against Phil's angry diatribe that he is just a piece of equipment, Maxwell cautions, "you just don't understand. You let things bother you too much. I learned a long time ago, you can't let things bother you" (p. 284). The individual player comprehends the dehumanizing aspects of professional football but is impotent to do anything about them. The insult is twofold: first the player is thought of as merely a body with no intelligence or individuality of its own; and second, the body is thought of as commercial property to be used to maximize the success of the team, the machine as a whole. As Clinton Foote points out to Phil during his hearing, "we own you and you check with us when you want to do something, we don't check with you" (p. 298).

To keep the individual bodies in reasonable repair, the team hires expert physical therapists as trainers. But the opinions of these men mean little if they do not conform with the immediate needs of management. "As a result, a player who the trainers thought needed rest or even surgery often found himself shot full of Novocain facing a grinning Deacon Jones and the player was given the chance to exhibit the most desirable of traits —the ability to endure pain" (p. 168). Trainers are thus mere "technicians, line workers who repaired broken club property" (p. 168). The treatment of injuries, like salary negotiations or any other personnel problem, becomes a series of efficient tactical decisions designed to increase the return of corporate assets. The *team*, as Phil points out to Maxwell, is not the players, but the front office.

It becomes increasingly clear that if professional football is not playful it is because the sport is as mercenary as any giant business; its internal arrangements are duplications of an expedient, capitalist society. When Phil talks about the exhilaration of catching a football, his joy is real but transient. No play is possible beyond the momentary flashes Phil experiences in practice so long as play is intimately connected to a powerful bureaucracy which, because it is goal-directed, is itself antagonistic to play. "Games may well seduce us into purposiveness. Into wanting to win some-*thing*. But play: that is a different matter. Play is purposeless. Persons who play games in order to win are not playing games; they are working at them. That's why they do not win."[15]

The second major perversion of the play-attitude in *North Dallas Forty* is an inordinate emphasis on uncontrolled violence. There is no necessary contradiction between play and violence so long as the violence is bound by rules. Huizinga calls fighting "the most intense, the most energetic form of play and at the same time the most palpable and primitive."[16] He goes on to say that "the limits of licit violence do not necessarily stop at the spilling of blood or even at killing. The medieval tournament was always regarded as a sham-fight, hence as play, but in its earliest forms it is reasonably certain that the joustings were held in deadly earnest and fought out to the death, like the 'playing' of the young men before Abner and Joab."[17] So long as violence is limited and ordered by ritual or some other cultural function it may be susceptible to the play-attitude. But in *North Dallas Forty*, violence is never play. The supposedly licit violence of football is no more acceptable or playful than the violence outside the game.

The opening scene of the novel casts Phil as the fourth member of a dove hunting party which also includes Seth Maxwell, O. W. Meadows, and Jo Bob Williams. The hunt itself turns out to be a partly boring, partly terrifying bloodfest, and sets the tone for the entire novel. While hunting may well be a play function, on this expedition hunting doves involves all the strategy and finesse of proliferating the air with shotgun pellets. In addition to the doves, one of which has its head twisted off by Jo Bob, the group manages to slaughter five ducks, a field lark, an owl, and a cat. Most of the bodies are mutilated. Phil's horror during this episode does not arise from his inability to understand that "when you go hunting you are supposed to kill,"[18] as Dick Schaap has put it, but rather from his inability to fathom such indiscriminate, senseless violence. Surely there is a difference between hunting and slaughter. While hunting was originally not a sport at all, but a survival technique, today it is, ironically, one of the few sports which remain relatively uncommercialized. But as we have seen, the spirit of play is absolutely denied during the dove hunt. Nowhere do we see anything like the strategic pursuit of one's prey. The unconcerned mangling and mutilation and the killing of nonsporting animals shows us not a hunt at all, but murder in the form of a sadistic war against nature.

This illusory distinction between acceptable and unacceptable violence is at the heart of *North Dallas Forty*. One of the most appealing aspects of football to the spectator is its emphasis on permissible violence. Football's phenomenal rise in popularity coincides with a period in American history characterized by racial violence, mass student demonstrations, and, of course, the composite of horrors we call the Vietnam War. For the spectator, football may provide easy, vicarious victories in a world of less reliable possibilities. The exemplary fan finds some compensation in the good, "clean," legalized violence of football as opposed to the chaotic violence outside the game. Everything is done according to rules on the gridiron; a violation of the rules is a violation of the spirit and order of the game, and any infraction is therefore promptly penalized. In fact, in recent seasons, to fully satisfy the fans' sense of justice, the National Football League has adopted the practice of naming the "culprits" over the public address system. This strict meting out of punishment in professional football allows the spectator to assume that violence which is not penalized is not only legal, but also a part of the order of the game.

Peter Gent capitalizes on this tension between supposedly lawful violence and its illicit counterpart, and collapses them to show that they are interchangeable. The game is as antagonistic to play as the society at large because it is intrinisically tied to that society. Ultimately, the violence of the stadium is indistinguishable from the violence outside because both are utterly impersonal, unwarranted, absurd. And the source of much of the impersonality in *North Dallas Forty* is the status of professional football as a big business, governed by the scruples of the marketplace. A poignant example, which combines the impersonal violence of the game with the ethics of big business, takes place during the game with the Giants. Alan Claridge, one of Dallas's star rookie players, has a previously injured hamstring muscle buckle on him while returning a kickoff, "and as he fell forward Bobby Joe Putnam hit him full speed flush in the face with his headgear" (p. 257). The detailed description of Claridge's face is awesome. I quote the description at length to emphasize how naive is the attitude that there is anything like "good, clean fun" involved in such brutality: "he was covered with blood. His double bar mask was shattered and his face was swollen and discolored a purplish-black. . . . His nose was smashed flat and split open as if someone had sliced the length of it with a razor. The white cartilage shone brightly from the red-black maw that had been his nose. . . . He tried to say something, raising his hand, but it was lost in a gurgle as black blood poured from his mouth" (pp. 258-59). When informed of the extent of Claridge's injury, B. A.'s only response is an indifferent "Oh." We later learn that B. A. will probably place Claridge on injured waivers for the rest of the season. As Phil puts it, "he was merely a damaged part being replaced" (pp. 268-69).

Glimpses of the world outside professional football are transmitted through a daily stream of newspaper headlines and radio news. Phil connects several of the stories with the Kennedy assassination. That cataclysmic event in American history serves as a focal point for the violence of American life, here localized in Dallas, Texas. The news stories are also significant because they always point up the hypocrisy of American justice. One pair of headlines on Wednesday announces "a several-hundred-year prison sentence for possession of marijuana" and "a seven-year probation handed to a narcotics agent for kidnapping, sodomy assault, and murder with malice of his twenty-two-year-old stewardess girl friend" (p. 87). Dallas is also where a property owner is "acquitted of the murder of a sixteen-year-old boy who was stealing tools from his garage" (p. 73) and "a plainclothes police detective shot and killed a long-hair who made 'obscene and suspicious gestures' at the officer. The victim turned out to be a garage mechanic on his way home from work" (p. 104).

When the team arrives in New York for their Sunday game against the Giants, we find the headlines there are as violent as they were in Dallas. But in New York there is a difference. The pain and suffering we have witnessed in team practices and in following Phil Elliott throughout the week have become such pervasive metaphors for an entire society that by Saturday night Phil's "game plan" for Sunday becomes completely mingled with the blurbs of violence coming over the radio:

I undressed, slipped into bed and studied my game plan to the sounds of the eleven o'clock news. My sideline adjustment against a roll zone was a turn in. *A building was blown up in Greenwich Village.* Against any shooting linebacker or safety blitz all but two of my routes automatically changed to quick down and ins. *Two policemen were shot from ambush while answering a disturbance call.* All wide receivers must pull up on deep routes against a three deep defense. *Two plastic bombs were found in suitcases in lockers in the International Terminal at Kennedy.* I closed my book and watched the weather forecast: Cloudy and cool for Sunday. Everything was in order. [P. 224.]

The last sentence here adds an important irony to the passage. Chaotic violence has become so widespread in our society that the only way we can handle it is to pretend that somehow it is part of the "order" of life. We must never forget, as John McMurtry reminds us, that football fans and citizens are not different people. "The game inside the stadium and the game outside are as alike as the adoring roars that greet touchdowns and police powers."[19] Gent forcefully and persistently explodes the myth that the game is somehow different from the society which surrounds it. The violence of the game and the violence of the "real" world are insepar- able because those realms are irrefutably the same. Indeed, Allen Guttmann, in his fine book *From Ritual to Record: The Nature of Modern Sports*, argues convincingly that football is not cathartic for its spectators. Rather, fans are more likely to become violent than passive as a result of their vicarious experience of the game: "The role of shouting, screaming spectator compensates us for the more restrained roles of parent, employee, and citizen. And, if the excitement becomes excessive, it spills over into riotous behavior."[20]

It seems clear that the association of Dallas with the Kennedy assassination helps to centralize and highlight the violence implicit in so much of American life. Gent's realistic use of setting also helps to foster some other natural connections. As the center of the oil industry, Texas may readily be associated with money and large corporate enterprise. Additionally, Texas is home for some of the most phenomenally successful football organizations, notably the Dallas Cowboys and the University of Texas Longhorns. Each of these correlations, implicitly or explicitly made, is woven into the substance of the novel as an important aspect of theme. *North Dallas Forty* thus describes a society, both on and off the field, dominated by violence, racism, and football. For the white football hero there are millionaire businessmen always willing to supply girls, understanding policemen willing to tear up a speeding ticket, and endlessly patient creditors ready to extend credit indefinitely as long as one remains on the active roster.

North Dallas Forty elaborates a world gone football crazy, where potential play has been perverted by an emphasis on rigid conformity, excessive violence, and vicarious experience. The last of these perversions encounters them all because it is a direct product of the commercialization of the game, which in turn ties the game inextricably to the society as a whole. Except in occasional flashes on the field, reality is never played in *North Dallas Forty*; it is manipulated and controlled by ultimate football groupies like Conrad Hunter, who considers his players members of his "family." Having made two hundred million dollars, Conrad can now afford the luxury of hanging out in locker rooms. Football is a vicarious fantasy world transmitted through television every Sunday to forty million fans hoping "to escape themselves and their wretched lives" (p. 213). And football is an exemplary sport through which the spectator may make that escape. Because it emphasizes direct physical violence, because it encourages heroic measures of strength and speed, because the game is played out against an irreversible clock, football provides the fan with a vicarious experience which has the intensity of modern life and heroic proportions unavailable to most spectators in their own lives. The game becomes a kind of sublimation for the pent-up energies of the fan who endures the aggressive competitiveness of the business world. In a remark which once again ties football to the violence of the society at large, Phil points out that "that surplus of energy is the cause of crimes of passion and spectator sports" (p. 192).

Through their identification with the values of the game—strength, speed, violence, agressiveness—fans are able to participate in a heroic world. *North Dallas Forty* is full of men like Steve Peterson, Louis Lafler, and Bob Beaudreau, rich male hangers-on who love nothing better than to pander to their favorite ballplayers in exchange for license to inhabit the world of professional football. For Phil, they remain just another of the game's anomalies: "It was always surprising to me to see respected businessmen who deal in millions of dollars and thousands of lives giggling like pubescent schoolgirls around a football player" (p. 70). They are always ready to supply "dollies," as Peterson puts it, and they literally like nothing better than hanging around football players, trying through social intercourse and financial favors to make themselves part of the heroic world they are used to seeing on the football field. Of course, the impulse is vicarious and the satisfactions are illusory. The irony of Louis Lafler's giggling around football players is that his own business success depends upon the same aggressiveness and corporate efficiency demanded by Dallas football. Lafler, Beaudreau, and Peterson do not want to be part of the *organization* of professional football; they are already integral parts of that world. What they want to identify with is the game on the field.

But where does the player escape to? Acutely aware of how well-packaged the game is, the player realizes that he plays at the whim of men like Conrad Hunter, who think a player's race (crowd appeal) and his religion and malleability (personal appeal) are more important than his ability. It is no wonder then that football players live with intense and constant fear. One potential escape, and one which offers the possibility of play, is love.

The unhappy evidence of *North Dallas Forty* is that love and sex are no more playlike than football; furthermore, like football, they are often perverted from direct to vicarious experience. There is not a single example of a happy marriage in the novel. Most of the sexual activity in the book is tainted by boorishness and chauvinism. Jo Bob, Alan Claridge, and Andy Crawford often resort to sexual violence and exhibitionism, brutalizing and embarrassing their own dates and anyone else who happens to be accessible. Perhaps the most telling moment of the novel comes when Maxwell and Phil mutually decide that neither has ever really loved anyone. This vacuum of real emotion suits Maxwell extremely well. He likes nothing better than a nightly escapade of sexual marauding and then being able to recount his adventures in his curiously personal style—the "fuck" story. "It was as if the experience hadn't really happened and he couldn't really feel it until he recounted it to someone and watched and listened to their reaction. Until he talked about it, it wasn't real" (p. 151). Here we see the same kind of vicarious quality applied to sexual experience that football has for the society as a whole. It is as if Maxwell, once tempered by the fantasy world of televised football, must submit all his experience to the same kind of cinematic replay. And so Phil provides the valuable function of being an audience for Maxwell's stories.

In spite of the emotional sterility of *North Dallas Forty*, we sense in Phil a desire to feel more genuinely, to transcend the futility of his environment. While he remains a willing audience for Maxwell's stories, there is a note of despair in his conclusion that he has never really loved anyone. Phil remains detached from the sexual violence of post-game parties, Claridge's exhibitionism, and Peterson's "dollies." Except for Maxwell, with whom he shares a very dubious "brotherhood of mutilation," Phil remains curiously aloof from his teammates. In nightclubs and at parties where the antics of Crawford, Claridge, and Jo Bob are predictably uncouth, he remains physically isolated as well as emotionally detached. For example, after arriving at a party at Andy Crawford's we catch Phil in a typical pose, isolated from his fellows by choice: "I slipped into the kitchen. I hopped my butt up onto the drainboard and sat watching the party through a hole . . ." (p. 17). The environment is so oppressive that even a player is more often reduced to a spectator.

Ironically, it is through Bob Beaudreau, who represents the violence, racism, and hypocrisy of a whole society, that Phil first meets Charlotte Caulder at Crawford's party. One thing which they immediately share is a distaste for the troglodytic goings-on at the party. But while Charlotte is incredulous that men like Peterson "supply" the ballplayers with women, Phil remains cynical and calmly explains the principles of "groupie-ism." The scene is repeated two nights later at Rock City, this time in public, with Claridge exposing himself on stage, calling his date a whore, and going through the motions of masturbating. Phil and Charlotte leave before a full-scale riot breaks out. In every way Charlotte is different from the people Phil typically meets through the ballclub. Significantly, she does not live in Dallas, but on a cattle ranch in Lacota fifty miles away. As if in open contempt of the racism of Beaudreau and the Dallas football management, she lives with David Clarke, a black writer friend from her college days.

It would be a mistake to overemphasize the depth of Phil's relationship with Charlotte since it is never really fulfilled. Their relationship remains a potentiality. But therein lies its significance, too. What Charlotte represents more than anything else is an alternative to all the values we associate with the big business of professional football: impersonal violence and manipulation, racism, hypocrisy, emotional sterility—a world where the direct, physical, and liberating experience of play has been perverted into a commercial theater which emphasizes the vicarious experience of millions of spectators rather than the potentially transcendent experience of the player himself. Charlotte realizes that football has made Phil "a very mean man." Phil's lovemaking shows the isolation and detachment cultivated over years in an environment where fear and pain are the key emotions. Charlotte holds the promise of a future filled with sincerity, feeling, maybe love. There is something genuinely unpretentious about her offer to have Phil move out to the ranch. She recognizes as fully as Phil the insanity of the world, but in her private way she is surviving a lot better than he is. Her proposal is simple and yet appealing: "I have plenty of money and you have a measure of success. Instead of starting with a one-room flat and slowly growing apart in pursuit of life in the seventies, we start with everything and whittle it down to each other. That's how we would live in this insane world" (p. 194).

Although isolated from the urbanity of Dallas, Charlotte's ranch is an authentic place, a place of physical work, the only spot in *North Dallas Forty* which has the visceral reality that ought to be available on the football field. There are few scenes in the novel as vivid as the one in which Charlotte and David deftly castrate a young bull. Phil is astonished by the whole procedure, which elicits from him his most emotional response before the climactic scene of the novel: " 'Jesus—Jesus—Jesus— Jesus!!' I moaned' 'JEEESUS!' " (p. 189). This is the only authentic experience in the novel besides catching a football.

From Maxwell's "fuck" stories to Claridge's exhibitionism, to Conrad Hunter's "groupie-ism," to Sunday's forty million football fans, *North Dallas Forty* is a picture of indirect experience completely replacing direct participation. It is a world where individuals borrow their identities rather than creating them. Ironically, the mundane experience of physical work on Charlotte's ranch is closer to the play impulse than all the tendencies associated with professional football. Charlotte's ranch represents the challenge, if not of play, at least of direct experience. It is a place where the individual can create his own values and identity instead of having them dictated to him by front office personnel. Increasingly, the world we tend to call "real" has become vicarious.

The last two scenes of the novel reinforce this deeply ironic view of American life. In the penultimate scene Phil is expelled from professional football because he smokes dope. We realize that this is only the technical reason (Emmett Hunter smokes, too). He's been sleeping with the boss's fiancée, and, more than that, he refuses to submit to the total control that management insists upon. His real crime is refusing to becomes a machine, insisting as he did with Maxwell, that the game should still be "fun." The naiveté of dichotomizing work and play is pointed up here. Our concept of the "game" increasingly becomes the cat-and-mouse affair that takes place between the individual and the forces which seek to control him. That is why center Bill Schmidt pleads with Phil and Maxwell to convince Conrad Hunter that he did not support the player's strike. Being a member of Conrad's "family" really means being part of his machine. And so Phil, freed from the manipulation of professional football, sees that "the game wasn't on the field, it never had been" (p. 304). The real game is in the offices of management. The only rules that count are those prescribed by club owners, business managers, directors of player personnel, and head coaches—the stockholders of the corporation. As Phil puts it, "I had been trapped on a technicality that explained the ultimate pointlessness of the life I had been living. . . . I hadn't been beaten and I hadn't quit. I had been disqualified" (p. 304).

In the final scene of the novel, in which Beaudreau slaughters Charlotte Caulder and David Clarke, all the horrific tendencies in *North Dallas Forty* come together. Again, Charlotte and David represent flexibility and openmindedness. With one clip of his Magnum .357 Beaudreau blows them and their liberal values to bits. Charlotte and David will become just another of Dallas's terrifyingly violent headlines. When Phil explodes in a rage of horror and tries to kill Beaudreau, it is Beaudreau who says that *Phil* is crazy. For the first time in the novel we begin to believe him. Sanity in this novel requires racism, violence, and hypocrisy, all the same values which professional football in particular and America in general harbor. There is nothing a puny individual like Phil Elliott can do about it. The ultimate irony of the novel is that this "justice" will win out in both sport and society. As the sheriff says of Beaudreau, "'Well, we found a lot of marywana in the gal's room, and what with him findin' her with the nigger. If he jest buy hisself a good lawyer he'll probably be all right.'" (p. 314). This is why it is not really important to define Charlotte and Phil's relationship; it remains a never-to-be-fulfilled possibility. What *is* significant is that she represents an alternative to Beaudreau and his values, and that Beaudreau destroys her.

North Dallas Forty turns out to be as reductive as *Fat City*. Despite the glamor and money of professional football, the price one must pay for success is to sacrifice the freedom, joy, and creativity of the player for the conformity and rigidity of the machine. Direct experience and flexibility are everywhere sacrificed for vicarious experience and manipulation. The triumphant values of *North Dallas Forty* are violent, hypocritical, inhumane. It is appropriate then that the final image of the novel has Phil looking out over the silent rolling pasture "listening for sounds of life in the distance."

CHAPTER FOUR

"END ZONE"

Play at the Brink

The critical juxtaposition of *North Dallas Forty* and *End Zone* marks an interesting transition in this study, for while both books use football as a major focus, football suggests, radically different metaphors in each. In *North Dallas Forty* professional football is a direct reflection, indeed a microcosm, of contemporary America. As we move on to *End Zone* the violence so prevalent in *North Dallas Forty* becomes much more implicit and potential than actual, but also much more horrible. Lurking behind the desperation of the season of a college football team is the imagery of holocaust and apocalypse conjured by the possibility of nuclear war. Indeed, "apocalypse" is one of the new words which Gary Harkness adds to his vocabulary as part of his daily ritual. The figure of the "end zone" is only marginally important as an image of the goal line on a football field—the finite territorial objective of every offensive series of plays. Like Barth's image of "the end of the road," "end zone" becomes a metaphor for a much more ambiguous and ultimate end which symbolizes the disintegration of modern life.

Still, the apocalyptic vision of *End Zone* has some striking and surprising implications for the possibility of play in this world. In *North Dallas Forty* organized football is connected to a closely detailed, realistic conception of society. Since both the larger society and professional football are overwhelmingly ruled by an inflexible technology, by the metaphor of the computer, and by the triumph of vicarious over direct experience, the freedom of play is only fleetingly possible and cannot be recovered. In *End Zone* as long as sport is tied to a literal presentation of the barren world of the Texas plains, it too remains unplayful. There is nothing creative, free, or joyous about Logos College football. But the imminent chaos of *End Zone* seems to cause so much strain that there are some cracks in the enveloping mechanical order which so tightly rules *North Dallas Forty*. The play-attitude, consequently, emerges unexpectedly in the form of spontaneous and primitive games which appear as much more playful accompaniments to the menacing threat of nuclear holocaust. Play is not only possible in *End Zone*, but it is also partially recovered. The novel thus poses the choice of a society at the brink: total regimentation in a world of technology or a return to a more primitive, ritualized past to recover the play-attitude.

Essential to any mythos of football is an understanding of the game's territorial nature. Football has many striking similarities to conventional warfare in which territorial aggrandizement is the key to victory. The hash marks on the field are fairly literal battle lines, and, as so many commentators have reminded us, the language of football reflects the terminology of warfare. Games are won and lost in the "trenches" or the "pit"; quarterbacks throw "aerials" and "bombs"; defensive strategy often calls for the "blitz" or "zone" coverage. Even the names of the various positions reflect the agonistic nature of the game: "flankers," "guards," "tackles," and "safeties." Enough has been said about the violence of the game in connection with *North Dallas Forty* to make that aspect of football sufficiently clear.

It also seems clear that the incredible complexity of football makes it a very modern, a very technological game. But there are several other important aspects of football which make it an appropriate theme for the apocalyptic vision of *End Zone*. Murray Ross has pointed out the importance of the time element in football. Unlike sports such as baseball, tennis, golf, or bowling, football is played against the clock. "Time in football is wound up inexorably until it reaches the breaking point in the last minutes of a close game. More often than not it is the clock which emerges as the real enemy, and it is the sense of time running out that regularly produces a pitch of tension uncommon in baseball."[1] In any sport there are sudden reversals, and upsets, but in football the "potential for sudden disaster or triumph is as great . . . as it is in our own age, and although there is something ludicrous in equating interceptions with assassinations and long passes with moon shots, there is something valid and appealing in the analogies."[2] In other words, football is a game which encourages cataclysm and thus mirrors the uncertainty and frailty of our lives better than, say, baseball, which in its pastoral vision encourages a stopping of time and a retreat to our rural past.

The signs of imminent chaos are everywhere in *End Zone*. Nuclear holocaust is one of Gary's daily fantasies as he imagines different cities destroyed by modern disaster technology. The English language, once a source of creativity, expressiveness, and poetry, is rapidly disintegrating into a collection of clichés, jargon, and abstract technical language. In a world of vast uncertainty what is the source of order, if any order at all is possible? What kind of god presides over this imminent destruction? What relevance does the play-attitude have to a vision of the world so fantastic and apocalyptic? In the final chapter of *Homo Ludens*, Huizinga gives an often-bitter appraisal of the decadence of the play-attitude in "contemporary civilization." And the French play theorist, Roger Caillois, who rarely agrees with most of the play theorists cited in this work, concurs with Huizinga on this point at least. Caillois notes the "regression" of the play-attitude in the modern world: "It is a world that is not sacred, without festivals, without play, therefore, without fixed moorings, without devotional principles, without creative license, a world in which immediate interest, cynicism, and the negation of every norm not only exist, but are elevated into absolutes in place of the rules that underlie all play, all noble activity, and honorable competition. One should not be surprised to meet there few things that do not lead to war."[3]

For Caillois, war is the ultimate consequence of all the profanations of honorable competition, rule-governed behavior, and play activity in the modern world. His writing after World War II perhaps gives him some justification for the bitter tone of his later work. But Caillois's charge is a serious one, one which cannot be taken lightly in view of our experience of such things as Hiroshima. It thus seems appropriate to begin a study of the play-element in *End Zone* with Delillo's treatment of nuclear war.

Huizinga was the first play theorist to study elaborately the play element in warfare. As he says, "all fighting that is bound by rules bears the formal characteristics of play by that very limitation."[4] Throughout his discussion of play and war, Huizinga emphasizes the necessity for the play-attitude of antagonists who regard each other as equals, if we are to consider their fighting a ludic function. Thus he concludes that surprise attacks, ambushes, raids, and mass exterminations are nonagonistic. In such forms of combat there are no rules, no sense of equality exists, and no possible cultural, religious, or ritual purposes may be served. Huizinga wrote *Homo Ludens* before the specter of nuclear warfare became a real possibility. And so although he spoke of modern warfare as seeming to have "hardly any trace of the old play-attitude" we may want to ask how much more intense might his attitude have been if *Homo Ludens* had been written after Nagasaki. The key word here is "seeming," for Huizinga brilliantly perceived that all human activity is permeated by the play-attitude. In spite of the fact that modern warfare violates international law and "flouts" the code of honor, it is not completely free of "the old play-attitude." "Politics are and always have been something of a game of chance; we have only to think of the challenges, the provocations, the threats and denunciations to realize that war and the policies leading up to it are always, in the nature of things, a gamble, as Neville Chamberlain said in the first days of September 1939. Despite appearances to the contrary, therefore, war has not freed itself from the magic circle of play."[5]

Nuclear war, perhaps even more than conventional warfare, depends on the element of surprise. It guarantees mass death and may mean the destruction of civilization. How can we square such ultimate disaster with the play-attitude? Again, Huizinga gives us the answer, and *End Zone* supports him. The "gameness" of even a nuclear war is found in its "challenges, provocations, threats and denunciations."[6] In fact, the potential consequences may well lead to making nuclear war even more of a contest than World War II. Major Staley prophesies a "not-too-distant-future" in which "humane" wars will be fought.

Each side agrees to use clean bombs. And each side agrees to limit the amount of megatons he uses. In other words we'll get together with them beforehand and there'll be an agreement that if the issue can't be settled . . . then let's make certain we keep our war as relatively humane as possible. So we agree to use clean stuff. And we actually specify the number of megatons; let's just say hypothetically one thousand megs for each side. So then what we've got is a two-thousand-megaton war. We might go further and say we'll leave your cities alone if you leave ours alone. . . . So right off the bat you avoid the fallout hazard and millions of bonus kills, or deaths from fallout. And at the same time you eliminate city-trading and punishing strikes against the general population. Of course the humanistic mind crumbles at the whole idea. It's the most hideous thing in the world to these people that such ideas even have to be mentioned. But the thing won't go away. The thing is here and you have to face it. [Pp. 63-64.]

We cannot help but notice the play-element in this description. Major Staley's prophecy for humane wars necessitates the adherence to *rules.* Instead of a few men "flinging mud all over the planet" nuclear wars of the future may have to be very deliberate and cautious because of the imposition of rules. As Staley concludes, "There'd be all sorts of controls. You'd practically have a referee and a timekeeper. Then it would be over and you'd make your damage assessment" (p. 64). And although I would not under any circumstances call nuclear warfare a truly ludic function, Delillo's description of the application of play-elements to potentially cataclysmic events stresses that those game features may indeed make the destructive possibilities more controllable. The technology which replaced the play-attitude in *North Dallas Forty* seems to have given rise to a new, albeit a dangerous, play-sphere.

Gary and Major Staley play a simulated war game one night in the Major's motel room. Although the Major has obviously spent a great deal of time planning the game situation, devising even the most particular maps and charts, several problems detract from the quality of the play experience. First of all, Gary is hardly a worthy opponent for the Major. We know that Gary is fascinated by disaster technology and that he is easily the best student in Major Staley's course in Aspects of Modern Warfare, but he has no experience in the "manipulations, both diplomatic and military, which might normally precede any kind of large-scale destruction" (p. 183). The game is thus played, initially, between unequal opponents, one of the most important violations of the play-spirit for Huizinga.

A second manifest problem with the Major's war game is one common to all war games—"the obvious awareness on the part of all participants that this wasn't the real thing" (p. 180). This is an important point, for the activity which we label play must be compelling enough while it is going on not to betray any inferiority to so-called reality. As Eugen Fink reminds us, "Each game is an attempt at existence, a vital experiment that encounters in the play-thing the essence of unyielding reality."[7] It is naive on the Major's part to declare that "the gaming environment . . . could never elicit the kind of emotions generated in times of actual stress" (pp. 180-81). Perhaps the emotions are more intensely felt during a political showdown like the Cuban Missile Crisis, but surely they are the *same* emotions felt during a war game, and surely both situations elicit *real* emotions. During the first part of the war game, in which he elaborately builds the scenario of conflict, Major Staley is correct. Gary is completely dependent upon the Major's explanations. He cannot feel the tension inherent in the game situation because, unlike the true player who is the lord of his creations, he has had no share in the creative functions of the game. And the Major, who has expressed his creativity in planning the game, cannot experience the joy of play because his opponent is unworthy.

The second part of the game, however, is quite different. Gary becomes an active participant in this segment of the game, planning his strategy, and sharing in the challenges, provocations, and direct attacks which are intrinsic play elements in a war game. Both players become totally absorbed in the gravity of the situation they are resolving. "There were insights, moves, minor revelations that we savored together. Silences between moves were extremely grave. Talk was brief and pointed. Small personal victories (of tactics, of imagination) were genuinely satisfying. Mythic images raged in my mind" (p. 184). Although only twelve moves are required to complete the game, these twelve moves are made over a period of more than three hours. It is not so much the thought of winning or losing which dicates the seriousness of the game and its slow, strategic pace, but rather the gravity of the situation itself. The players here are completely immersed in a world they are creating with every move, and that is why the game is both real and totally compelling. At the completion of the twelfth move, "the telephone rang. Major Staley turned quickly in his chair, terrified for a long second, and then simply stared at the commonplace black instrument as it continued to ring" (p. 185). It is almost as if the first ring of the telephone strikes the Major's ears as a bomb exploding. His terror is real because the game is real and because, completely caught up in the world of that game, his absorption is suddenly shattered. The mundane ("commonplace") world of reality has been utterly displaced by the greater game world.

It is difficult to determine whether move twelve actually resolves the conflict situation or renders one side helpless, but once the telephone rings the "magic circle of play," as Huizinga refers to the gaming environment, the total engagement of the players, for this game, has been destroyed forever. But we must not lose sight of the fact that while it lasted the game was an unyielding encounter with reality. For those who may be appalled by Staley's concept of "humane" warfare, perhaps it is not so much warfare that they do not understand as play. Play may be deadly serious indeed, and "cannot be defined by isolating it on the basis of its relationship to an *a priori* reality and culture."[8] Insofar as play is a basic existential phenomenon any activity may be played; indeed, other existential phenomena may themselves be played. Thus, as Fink has carefully pointed out, we may play at work, seriousness, love, reality, and play itself.⁹ We cannot, then, simply dismiss war as a nonludic function just because it is horrifying. However horrible warfare may be, its reality as described by Major Staley, and then enacted by Gary and the Major, conforms very closely to the play-attitude.

The image of the "end zone" hints at the disintegration of modern life. Nuclear holocaust is certainly the most cataclysmic sign of the breakdown in order in our world, but it is not the only such portent of chaos. As we have seen, even the specter of nuclear war can be made more manageable, more susceptible to order, if it is made part of the playsphere. At the heart of *End Zone* is the tension between a world where play is possible and the encroachment of a newer world so totally subsumed by technology that it seems to preclude the possibility of play. On the one hand we have a world of creative play functions—expressive and poetic language, games, rituals—and on the other a world of objects, abstract mathematical relationships, and computer technology. This tension is epitomized by the football game that is described in the middle section of the novel.

The big game takes place between Logos College and West Centrex Biotechnical Institute. Logos College is the perfect setting for *End Zone*, for the logos is the cosmic reason which gives order, purpose, and intelligibility to the world. It is the creative word of God, incarnate as Jesus Christ. In *End Zone* the Word must struggle against science and the machine; the machine wins. West Centrex, led by their mechanical quarterback, Telcon (he has no first name), overwhelms the more philosophical players of Logos. And this contest, coming at the exact center of the novel, serves as an organizational and thematic focus for our attention. The individual characters' rage for order—Bloomberg "unjewing" himself, Myna trying to escape the responsibilities of beauty, Taft's monkish retreat into his room—is mirrored in Delillo's almost obsessive concern with numbers. To repeat: the central struggle between the college of the Word and the institute of technology comes at the exact center of the novel. Before the West Centrex game Logos has defeated six opponents, scoring a total of 246 points and giving up 41. Thus Logos has averaged the exact number of points per game as the total scored by their six opponents. We are also told early in the novel that the team has forty-five active players. Norgene Azamanian dies early in the first section of the novel and Jimmy Fife is on the disabled list all season. That makes 47 players in all, and exactly 47 players are named in the course of the novel. This proliferation of characters ensures that we will not get too close to most of them, thus preserving the impersonality of the machine age and at the same time keeping the records absolutely orderly and exacting.

Delillo's penchant for numbers is a way of holding back imminent confusion. It is a form of his own artistic gaming which makes his writing more playful. The closest we can come to order in the modern world is through play. Play becomes the only meaningful way of transcending chaos. In a long parenthetical aside to the reader, Delillo announces this theme in some detail:

> The exemplary spectator is the person who understands that sport is a benign illusion, the illusion that order is possible. It's a form of society that . . . is organized so that everyone follows precisely the same rules . . . ; that roots out the inefficient and penalizes the guilty; that tends always to move toward perfection. The exemplary spectator has his occasional lusts, but not for warfare. . . . No, it's details he needs—impressions, colors, statistics, patterns, mysteries, numbers, idioms, symbols. Football, more than other sports, fulfills this need. It is the one sport guided by language, by the word signal, the snap number, the color code, the play name. The spectator's pleasure, when not derived from the action itself, evolves from a notion of the game's unique organic nature. Here is not just order but civilization. [Pp. 89-90.]

If sport is the "benign" illusion that order is possible, one might assume that war is its malignant counterpart. The more we submit warfare to the play-attitude, requiring equal opponents, rules, and limitations, the closer we may come to Staley's concept of humane warfare. It thus becomes apparent that the military analogies delineated at the beginning of this chapter must remain mere analogies. The closer one gets to football the clearer it is that football is *not* warfare, because our present concept of warfare has a very different kind of territoriality from football's. Nuclear wars are not fought in the trenches. War may once have been the ultimate test of individual bravery, but as Gary and Major Staley prove, nuclear warfare is a slow, deliberate, agonizingly strategic game, much more like chess with its psychological ploys than football. As Alan Zapalac says, "I reject the notion of football as warfare. Warfare is warfare. We don't need substitutes because we've got the real thing" (p. 89). We do.

The notion of football as a form of order needs closer inspection, especially as it compares with Staley's war game. The terrifying reductivism of *End Zone* is pointed up by Creed's notion of football as a metaphor for life. If it is possible to consider Logos College as a small world unto itself, Creed may be seen as a god figure. Creed is famous "for creating order out of chaos," a feat he performs by building championship football teams. At practice sessions Creed never coaches from the sidelines, but stands aloof in a specially built tower high above the playing field. His godlike nature is reinforced by his role as "maker of plays, name giver" (p. 110). He is the creator of both plays and the names of plays, and his is the ultimate power to deny his players the words they need. One may question that it is only in the most limited of worlds that such an analogy may hold. But that is precisely the kind of narrowing Delillo would have us accept. As his name implies, Creed gives his players a code to live by, a creed they may cherish as so basic that one *must* live by it: Football is only a game, but it is the only game. How much more reductive can one get than that? One of the basic themes of this study is that the essential nature of reality is that it is played, that play is a basic existential phenomenon which confronts all the others. It has already been noted that the more fully a phenomenon—even one as potentially chaotic as nuclear war—may be made susceptible to the play-attitude, the more orderly it may become. But if the price of order is that the "only game" is football, then one can only conclude that that order is horrifyingly limited at best, meaningless at worst. And indeed, Delillo tells us that it is only a "benign illusion." Creed's motto is another sign that we have come perilously close to the "end zone."

On a smaller scale, most of the characters in *End Zone* are striving for a greater sense of order in their lives. As with the football metaphor, Delillo implies that order is only possible in the most finite and limited of lives.

Taft Robinson, like his namesake Jackie, is a player who breaks the color line. He is the first black ever to attend Logos College. He does so because Creed offers him "nothing but work and pain." Like Ellison's Invisible Man, Taft is trying to understand his black identity, and through the pain that comes of such understanding to create a new and orderly life for himself. And, as a further parallel with Ellison's character, Taft goes into seclusion at the end of the novel. Football was just a necessary rite of passage for Taft during which he learned to understand his black-ness more fully. For example, we catch him at one point reading a "gray" history book, sitting on a "gray" blanket, dressed in a white shirt, gray pants, and black socks. "He enveloped his presence in neutral shades. (A somber cream covered the walls and ceiling.) In his austerity he blended with the shadowless room, reading his gray history, a dreamer of facts" (p. 157). By the end of the novel, Taft is even more austere. He seems to have resolved completely any and all conflicts he may have had, and he is totally satisfied with his severely limited environment. Taft becomes monkish, but his surroundings are no longer gray. As if to emphasize his complete withdrawal into himself and his environment Taft now wears dark glasses and has shaved his head. His words are dressed in "black satin" and he turns to face the "black stone of Abraham" to pray. The room is fixed up just the way he wants it, with "just the right number of objects," and each object "exactly where it should be" (pp. 196-97). Gary recites the names of the individual objects, and almost like a computer print-out, Taft explains their significance. Taft's room may be an ordered environment, but the price for that order is a world stripped of emotion and productivity. It is a world of monkish austerity and seclusion. It is a world of objects arranged with geometric precision. It is a totally mechanical world stripped entirely of the element of play, and if it is orderly, it is also completely uninteresting.

Myna Corbett has come to the desert wasteland of Logos College to escape the responsibilities of beauty. At first we probably find her attitude admirable, both because of her refusal to give in to social pressures and her zany response to conventionality. But we soon learn that Myna, as her name implies, is a parrot. She is not a social revolutionary who refuses to lose weight or clear up her blemishes on principle. She is merely *afraid* to face the responsibilities of beauty, not *scornful* of them. Myna is not capable of espousing exciting or new ideas; she is only capable of parroting the ideas of others, like the incredible Mongolian science fiction writer, Tudev Nemkhu, who lives in Libya and writes exclusively in German. When Myna returns from Christmas vacation she is twenty pounds lighter and suddenly wearing ordinary clothes. Her explanation to Gary typifies her banality and appropriately concludes her "cop-out": " 'I had to do it, Gary. It became a question of self-definition. I was just moping along like an unreal person. I used to look forward to nothing-type things. I never really faced my own reality' " (p. 187).

The "nothing-type things" which Myna used to look forward to—breadless sandwiches; outrageous clothing which accentuated the worst parts of her figure; a commune in Mexico with Gary, the Chalk sisters, and a Rolls Royce—are the precise reasons why Gary was originally fascinated by her. When she returns from Christmas vacation twenty pounds lighter, he does not know how to react to the change. The Chalk sisters insist that he commit himself one way or another about Myna's new look. After Myna's long speech of self-justification Gary nebulously replies, " 'It's all very existential' " (p. 188). Esther Chalk's rejoinder keynotes an essential theme of the novel: "'Don't use words,' Esther said. 'Either you like her this way or you don't. You can't get out of it with words'" (p. 188). Although Esther is generally portrayed as an inane character, her remarks here are very much to the point. The breakdown of the social order implied by the possibility of nuclear war and made specific in the identity problems of the novel's individuals is mirrored in the debasement of the language.

If we accept the idea that language serves both creative and communicative functions, that it helps us to order our lives and our world, indeed to create them, then *End Zone* proclaims the disintegration of an expressive language. In *End Zone* the poetic content (and I use the word *poetic* in the broadest sense imaginable) of the language has been stripped away, still another manifestation of the loss of the play-attitude. Huizinga is a useful reference on this point: "All poetry is born of play: the sacred play of worship, the festive play of courtship, the martial play of the contest, the disputatious play of braggadocio, mockery and invective, the nimble play of wit and readiness. How far is the play-quality of poetry preserved when civilization grows more complicated?"[10] Judging by the evidence of *End Zone*, it is not preserved at all. Notice that Huizinga does not mention the "synchronic" play of computerized information in the list above. Nor does he mention the "reflexive" play of clichés. These are two of the strongest indictments Delillo makes against the current state of the language.

There is an obsessive concern with defining words and concepts in *End Zone*, as if reality can be fixed in some small way if it is defined. The problem is that the definitions given in *End Zone*, which are always brought forth spontaneously, are either so analytical that they tell us nothing about the nature of the thing being defined, or they are so abstract as to be meaningless. A few examples may help. In the middle of the Centrex game, amidst the screaming and yelling of his teammates, Jerry Fallon, for absolutely no apparent reason, spits out the following definition: "'Bed,' Jerry Fallon said. 'Pillow, sheet, blanket, mattress, spring, frame, headboard'" (p. 99). This is marvellous banter for the bored bench-warmer. In the desert one must concentrate on objects to breach the silence of wasted places. Such a definition takes the object completely apart and yet says absolutely nothing about what one might do with a bed.

At least Jerry Fallon's definition has a measure of precision and is fathomable. If one would know a thing by its parts then his definition is satisfactory, although one still wonders why he gave it in the first place.

I submit that the computer technology so pervasive in *North Dallas Forty* has gotten out of control in the more apocalyptic book, *End Zone*. More often, there is nothing like the objective precision of Jerry Fallon's definition, but rather a definition so abstract and mathematical that it *is* unfathomable. There is never any warning that such computerized information is forthcoming. One never knows what the key word is until it has already been spoken. Tim Flanders mentions the word *identity* in describing his grandfather, and at the end of that sentence Buddy Shock responds with this gem: " 'Identity,' Buddy Shock said. 'An equality satisfied by all possible values of the variable for which the standardized expressions involved in the equality are quantitatively determined." (pp. 44-45). This is obviously the most mathematical and abstract definition of the word and has nothing whatever to do with Tim Flanders' grandfather.

Dennis Smee talks about his "function" as co-captain of the team, and Billy Mast continues as follows: " 'Function,' Billy said. 'A rule of correspondence between two sets related in value and nature to the extent that there is a unique element in one set assigned to each element in the corresponding set, given the respective value differences' " (p. 122). Fortunately, Smee pays no attention to Billy Mast or he would never figure out how a co-captain is supposed to act. Finally, Champ Conway, the team's budding entomologist, is explaining the dangers of radioactive fallout to the "balance" of nature when Jimmy Fife adds this definition to our vocabulary: " 'Balance,' Fife said. 'The equality of effective values with respect to the applied number of reduced symbolic quantities on each side of an equation, excluding combined derivatives' " (p. 170). No one ever asks for mathematical definitions such as these, nor does anyone apparently pay any attention to them. They are all so abstract as to be chaotic rather than meaningful, and they are always given purely reflexively, as if the individuals who produce them were computers programmed to respond to certain key words.

Larger concepts are also described in purely abstract terms. For Creed, football is an "interlocking of systems." And for Gary, "History is the angle at which realities meet" (p. 35). The danger in such definitions, of course, is that one may concentrate on the "angles" and forget all about the "realities." Gary would have us believe that history is the "placement of bodies. What men say is relevant only to the point at which language moves masses of people or a few momentous objects into significant juxtaposition. After that it becomes almost mathematical" (p. 35). Such is the way one molds the modern militarist, to borrow Paul Hoch's phrase, and in doing so inures him to the poetic, expressive, indeed all the playful, aspects of language. Language, which in its ritual and naming functions can be used to create and to play reality, becomes a mechanical means of evading reality.

Gary is the only character in the novel who is at all disturbed that the language is becoming increasingly meaningless. Are we like the strange monadanom creature in Myna's science fiction novel? "It keeps making likenesses to make words. The words have no meaning. They're just fragments of cosmic language" (p. 140). Words *can* lose their meanings when they become too abstract. One of Gary's more intense moments in the desert comes when he sees "perhaps the one thing that did not betray its definition." "It was three yards in front of me, excrement, a low mound of it, simple shit, nothing more" (p. 69). The sight and the epiphany lead him to a long musing on the subject which concludes with the following ideas: "To begin to reword the overflowing world. . . . To re-recite the alphabet. To make elemental lists. To call something by its name and need no other sound" (pp. 70-71).

To call something by its name and need no other sound. Clearly, the language seems generally incapable of this task in *End Zone*. The true inspiration for the above train of thought is not really the mound of excrement Gary stumbles upon but the conversation he has just concluded with Major Staley on nuclear war. As Gary points out, there is "no way to express thirty million dead." The language is simply incapable of conjuring that much horror and death. Very much to the point of the present argument, Gary indicts our words as follows: " 'They don't explain, they don't clarify, they don't express. They're painkillers. Everything becomes abstract' " (p. 66). The true painkillers are the clichés we constantly employ to escape the responsibility of using language to explain, clarify, and express ideas. There is no way to express thirty million dead because the numbers are mere abstractions, formulas for reality, not reality itself. During the Vietnam War, for example, most Americans became inured to the idea of staggering death tolls. After years of weekly casualty statistics, the figures, instead of representing bodies, became mere numbers to most people.

Gary reminds us very early in the novel that "most lives are guided by clichés. They have a soothing effect on the mind and they express the kind of widely accepted sentiment that, when peeled back, is seen to be a denial of silence" (p. 54). When Norgene Azamanian and Tom Cook Clarke die they are eulogized with clichés. Norgene becomes "a fallen warrior" for whom "death had overwhelmed even his mediocrity and we [the team] conspired with his passing to make him gigantic" (p. 55). When the team learns that Mrs. Tom's plane has crashed they all react with exactly the same phrase. The cliché which guides Gary's father's life is a classic from the jargon of sports: When the going gets tough the tough get going. For Myna it is "the responsibilities of beauty," for Raymond Toon it is the trite jargon of sportscasting, and for Bobby Luke the idea which encapsulates his vision is his mindless desire "to go through a brick wall for Coach Creed." There is much to be said for Gary's insight that "perhaps it was easier to die than admit that words could lose their meaning" (p. 42).

Unfortunately, they can. Libby Margolis is calmed by the "incoherent doctrines" set forth in an economics textbook. Raymond Toon babbles indecipherable accounting phrases with no connecting explanations whatsoever. And the plays the football team uses have no discernible relationship to each other. Without certain key phrases it would take a genius to remember all the different plays. Delillo forewarns us that much of his game description will be "indecipherable," and indeed it is. A brief sampling of the plays will show how totally unrelated and enigmatic they are:

Twin option off modified crossbow.
Monsoon sweep, sting-in left, ready right.
Cradle-out, drill-9 shiver, ends chuff.
Middle-sift-W, alph-set, lemmy-2.
Delta-3 series, saddleback-in, shallow hinge reverse.
Zone set, triple tex, off-hit recon dive.
Twin deck left, ride series, white divide.
Blue turk right, double-slot, zero snag delay.
Gap-angle down, 17, dummy stitch. [Chapter 19.]

Notice that not one phrase is repeated. There are almost no distinguishable key words or numbers to indicate how the blocking on a play will develop or through which hole a running play should go. More importantly, the plays do not bear any apparent relationship to each other. In spite of the seemingly expressive phrasing, the above series of plays remains absolutely cryptic.

The only character besides our narrator who is at all interested in using language playfully is Wally Pippich, the public relations man. Pippich has a feel for sound; he knows, for example, that a name like Xerxes produces "a negative gut reaction." So he is going to promote the Logos College football team as a way of selling the school. His promotion will be head-lined by the following concept: "Taft Robinson and Gary Harkness. The T and G backfield. Taft and Gary. Touch and Go. Thunder and Gore" (p. 124). It would be easy to cite such linguistic dexterity as playful if not terribly sincere. Although Pippich's response to language bears some of the outward signs of play, he is certainly not a player. Robert E. Neale, in his *In Praise of Play: Toward a Psychology of Religion*, defines play as the religious response to the sacred. The realm of play is the realm of the sacred, and play is "psychologically defined as *any activity not motivated by the need to resolve inner conflict*."[11] Pippich, in Neale's terminology, is not a player but a "magician," a manipulator. He is a "pragmatist who desires the sacred to work for his own profane ends."[12] For Pippich admits that he does not know "squat" about football. The above phrasing comes purely from his feel for language and sound. Pippich is thus in danger of not only being literally off the mark with a phrase like "Thunder and Gore" but figuratively off as well. Thunder is as inappropriate to Taft as Gore is to Gary. An irresponsibly expressive language may there-fore be as meaningless as an overly mathematical and abstract one. The language of public relations, although outwardly playful, may be just as empty as the computer print-out.

There is still another danger in Pippich's language play. He has an un-canny habit of creating new words with "ation" endings, especially when he is excited about something. Scoop becomes "scoopation," big becomes "bigation," hand becomes "handation," and piss becomes "pissation." "Ation" is a suffix commonly associated with many of our more modern and technological words, such as transportation, aviation, and radiation. It is also a suffix which makes an abstract noun out of any word it com-pletes. Pippich makes an abstract object out of every word he subjects to this idiosyncrasy regardless of what part of speech it may have been originally. It is significant that he does not use such suffixes as "ish," "ly," "ic," or "al," all of which would make their words descriptive and relational rather than objective. The potential danger of Pippich's irrespon-sible quirk is that we might create through language an entire world of things, completely devoid of the descriptive relationships between those things, and thus a world where the poetic play of language would be impossible.

Perhaps what Delillo is really telling us is that in order to make our world more orderly, to ward off the impending chaos of the "end zone," we need to go backward rather than forward. Only in the more primitive and sacred functions of language will we discover its poetic nature. Huizinga tells us that "Poetry, in its original culture-making capacity, is born in and as play—sacred play, no doubt, but always, even in its sanctity, verging on gay abandon, mirth and jollity. There is as yet no question of the satisfaction of aesthetic impulse. This is still dormant in the experience of the ritual act as such, whence poetry arises in the form of hymns or odes created in a frenzy of ritual elation."[13] In many nontechnological cultures, sounds in the form of seed-syllables, not words, are the significant units of poetic and ritualized meaning. The "barriers imposed by all the allied sciences and disciplines" upon the study of exobiology, which Zapalac so energetically points out to his class, may well be read as a parable for the difficulties of the language itself: "multiple definitions . . . cross references nobody's even begun to put in any coherent form . . . terminologies which are untranslatable. . ." (p. 72). What we really need to do to recapture our reverence for language, as Zapalac says of his own discipline, is to "get into the mystery of it," to discover its most essential and sacred quality, the nuances of pure sound.

This emphasis on the primitive aspects of language is pointed up by the appearance of a very strange course at Logos College, a course in the untellable. The name of the course has a sacred ring to it. And we must remember that in primitive cultures the sacred is often that which is untellable. We have already seen that as we approach the "end zone" the language, because it becomes increasingly meaningless, is profaned. Insofar as the sacred may be defined as the opposite of the profane,[14] a sacred language may well be a meta-language of nondenotative sounds and gestures and silences which exist beyond the expression of words.

Billy Mast is the only football player who is taking the course, which consists of various language exercises in German, such as the memorization of Rilke's ninth Duino Elegy. Ignorance of German is a prerequisite for taking the course. The theme of the course may well be discerned from the choice of German for the language exercises: " ' I think the theory is if any words exist beyond speech, they're probably German words, or pretty close' " (p. 149). Once the words are stripped of their denotative meaning they are reduced to pure sound, in this particular case to Billy's "guttural struggle against those grudging consonants" (p. 58). One might express any of a whole range of emotions with such sounds, and it would only be the sound itself, not its definition, which would make the emotion expressed sincere or incongruous. This is pointed up by the fact that Billy "liked to hit his desk with both hands as he recited" (p. 58). One of the major activities of the class as a whole is to "shout in German a lot" (p. 148). The strong guttural sound of the words makes these responses appropriate. The danger of knowing the language is that one may confuse the meaning of a word with the sound it makes. Thus, after Billy Mast recites a few German words to himself he explains to Gary that "the German words gave him comfort, though not as much as they used to when he didn't know what they meant" (p. 116). We can see in Billy's desk banging and the class's shouting in German a primitive form of play. The words (here just nondenotative sounds) are made expressive, and thus meaningful, through gesture, pitch, stress, and volume. Part of the game would seem to be finding the most appropriate way to express nondenotative sounds. Once the meanings of the German words become known, the sounds must conform to those meanings and most of the creativity of the play-attitude is lost. In the untellable one creates and then plays a meta-language of sound and gesture to express meaning. If one already knows the language, pitch, stress, volume, and gesture may be imposed by preestablished denotative meanings; nothing is then created and there is no play.

We have a dramatic example of how much more expressive nondenotative sound may be than words, and how infinitely more playful one can be with them, in the only sexual scene of the novel. The scene is one in which Gary and Myna make love, with absolute appropriateness, in the stacks of the library. I quote the description at length to preserve the varieties of word, sound, and sexual play involved.

Myna looked different somehow. . . . She leaned toward the dictionary. We read the definitions to each other for a while. Some of them were extremely funny. Then we selected certain words to read aloud. We read them slowly, syllable by syllable, taking turns, using at times foreign or regional accents, then replaying the sounds, perhaps backward, perhaps starting with a middle syllable, and finally reading the word as word, overpronouncing slightly, noses to the page as if in search of protomorphic spoor. Some of the words put Myna into a state of mild delirium; she thought their beauty almost excessive. We kept reading for half an hour. The words were ways of touching and made us want to speak with hands. We went into a far corner of the high stacks. There I started taking off her dress. The great cumulus breasts came rolling out of hand-beaded blue Victorian velvet. . . . I made bubbling noises, rubbing my face in her breasts, scratching an itch just under my eye with her left nipple. Together we got the dress down over her hips, hitting each other lightly to warn the laughter off, and in time it was at her feet. I made strange noises of anticipation (*gwa, gwa*) and this made her hit me with both hands. . . . I plucked a chord or two on the tense elastic of her iridescent panties. . . .

We kissed and bit. . . . We touched, patted and licked. It may be impossible to explain why it seemed so very important to get her completely naked. Our hands rolled the pants past her hips and thighs. To mark the event I brought new noises to the room, vowel sounds predominating. Myna stepped away from the clothes, aware of the moment's dynamics, positing herself as the knowable word, the fleshmade sigh and syllable. [Pp. 178-79.]

The passage above is an apt justification of Huizinga's claim that "Frivolity and ecstasy are the twin poles between which play moves."[15] We notice here that verbal play gives way to physical play. What may have begun as frivolous word play becomes the only sexually expressive scene in the novel. We also notice that as the play becomes more physical, Gary's sounds become more primitive, both because the sounds are more expressive than words and because the words themselves are meaningless. There is a kind of backward evolution in this scene which symbolically retraces the gestation of language. Gary and Myna move from the dictionary definitions of words, to the syllables of those words, to purely expressive nondenotative sounds. The result of their play is to reach something substantial and tangible, something worthy of being represented by language, Myna, "positing herself as the knowable word, the fleshmade sigh and syllable" (p. 179).

The entire encounter has the aura of a primitive ritual. The emphasis here is certainly on the playfulness of foreplay, much like the ritualized courtship of less technological societies.[16] In *Fat City* and *North Dallas Forty* sexual activity and play are mutually exclusive. In *Fat City* sex is always thought of in terms of conquest or obligation. Sexual activity is thus always pursued in *Fat City* as a means of resolving conflict, and this is precisely the criterion that Robert E. Neal uses to define work, the psychological opposite of play.[17] For Neale, play arises out of a sense of harmony, not conflict. In *North Dallas Forty* sex for Phil Elliott is either completely abrupt and mechanical (with Joanne) or is a partial means of resolving the hostility he feels toward the Dallas football management (with Charlotte). When Phil arrives at Joanne's apartment she opens the door and says, "I was hoping we might fuck right now" (p. 79). The ensuing description of intercourse emphasizes the violence and pain of two large bodies manipulating each other; there is no foreplay at all. As for Gary and Myna in the library, their lovemaking is not at all "motivated by the need to resolve inner conflict."[18] The emphasis in the description is upon the playfulness of foreplay and not the intercourse itself. Indeed, the foreplay of this encounter is a kind of linguistic preening and strutting, more truly playful than any sexual episode in either *Fat City* or *North*

Dallas Forty. The conclusion seems to be that as we approach a social state of increasing chaos the way to make our sexual experience—like our experiences of war and language—more meaningful is to make it more playful.

We have stated earlier that the central tension in *End Zone* is between a world where play is possible and the encroachment of a newer world which seems to preclude the possibility of play. The newer world, which is amply represented by the debasement of the language, is consumed by automatism, technology, and routine. It is a world of "human xerography," as Gary calls it, in which repetition is a stay against chaos and an excuse for mindlessness and conformity. There is the spectacle of mass conformity so ludicrously described by Zapalac in his excoriation of flag-waving Shriners. And there are Texas state troopers filling out the accident report after Norgene Azamanian's automobile wreck. Rather than making an intensive inquiry into the circumstances of the accident, each trooper merely copies the same information his fellow troopers have already recorded. "One trooper stood writing, another at his shoulder writing what the first wrote. They checked each other out until it was apparent that they had reached an accord. It was a safeguard against errors and stray facts. There couldn't possibly be a mistake if they all had the same information" (p. 56). If the first trooper makes a mistake, that mistake will become a "verified" part of every trooper's report. Our supposed consolation that a misprogrammed computer may be corrected by human means is here denied by turning the humans into computers too.

In *End Zone* profane rituals abound as symptoms of an encroaching world where routine replaces play. Gary, Myna, and the Chalk sisters insist upon the importance of their picnics. But the picnics are just inane get-togethers which help pass the time in desolate West Texas. The Chalk sisters do nothing but argue with each other. Myna reads Tudev Nemkhu and babbles about driving a Rolls Royce to Mexico and forming a commune where they will eat enchiladas and oranges. And Gary just listens to all this drivel.

Bloomberg, in order to escape the emotional responsibility of his mother's death, paints a desert stone black as her grave marker instead of attending her funeral. Bloomberg's commitment to unjewing himself demands that he rid himself of what he calls the historical guilt of being Jewish. When Gary first sees the black stone in the desert he thinks, "Stone-painter. Metaphorist of the desert" (p. 33), as if some ritual in the desert had preceded his own. We learn much later that the stone is Bloomberg's mother's burial marker. It is an empty symbol of his determination to obliterate his cultural, linguistic, and emotional ties with his famiy heritage. One of the ways in which Bloomberg hopes to unjew himself is to "speak in complete sentences at least ninety-five percent of the time. Subject, predicate, object. It's a way of escaping the smelly undisciplined past with all its rid' alous customs and all its craziness—centuries of middle European anxiety and guilt" (p. 153). And Bloomberg is successful. The last time we see him his very ethnic name connotes no more to him "than the designation EK-seventeen might connote" (p. 153). As with Myna and Taft, Bloomberg's solution to his identity crisis is probably not very meaningful, and certainly not very interesting. He was a much more interesting character when, weighing 300 pounds, he felt like "an overwritten paragraph," just as Taft was more interesting displaying the spectacle of "black speed" on the football field, and Myna was more interesting escaping "the responsibilities of beauty." Anatole's ritualized burial of his mother is a profanation of his familial responsibility. His equation of Anatole Bloomberg with the designation EK-seventeen is one of the surest signs we have that the "end zone" must be imminent.

If anything can redeem the world from the technology, the automatism, the computerization, the empty rituals, the sterility of the "end zone" it is the play-attitude. Without the play-attitude the poetic and expressive functions of the language are lost, and even simple communication may break down. We have seen that even nuclear war may be made more controllable, more orderly, and less apocalyptic by subjecting it to the play-attitude. Amidst the host of meaningless rituals in *End Zone* there are also at least two other play-forms which transcend the profanity of these empty routines.

The first of these play-forms is the "Bang, You're Dead" game. Before the student body of Logos College returns to the campus for the fall semester the football players begin to play this "simple-minded" game which is a throwback to their childhoods. Like all games, "Bang, You're Dead" depends upon the adherence to rules: "your hand assumes the shape of a gun and you fire at anyone who passes. You try to reproduce, in your own way, the sound of a gun being fired. Or you simply shout these words: *Bang, you're dead.* The other person clutches a vital area of his body and then falls, simulating death. (Never mere injury; always death.) . . . You had to fall if you were shot. The game depended on this"

(p. 25). The emphasis in the game very quickly turns to the aesthetics of dying gracefully or acrobatically and killing selectively. There is only one "massacre," on the second day of the game, "when things were still shapeless." But the game is better than this, and has more potential than such unmitigated violence allows for. The "unwritten limits" which the game soon takes on make the game like a primitive ritual. All ritual is essentially played and depends upon strict adherence to forms and rules. Like "Bang, You're Dead," "ritual is . . . a matter of shows, representations, dramatic performances, imaginative actualizations of a vicarious nature.[19] Gary feels a mythic kinship between the game and its more primitive forms: "To kill with impunity. To die in the celebration of ancient ways" (p. 26).

"Bang, You're Dead" bears all the formal characteristics of play as defined by Huizinga: it is a voluntary activity; it is representational; it is governed by rules freely accepted by all players but absolutely binding upon them; it is "accompanied by a feeling of tension, joy and the consciousness that it is 'different' from 'ordinary life' "[20] The game is a way of breaking the isolation of the desert wasteland, "the middle of the middle of nowhere," as Gary parodies Gass's phrase (p. 24). The game depends upon this isolation; it is an essential quality of the play area. And so when the rest of the student body reports for classes the play-space is violated and the game must end. But its significance will not soon be forgotten, as Gary reminds us: "I would think of it with affection because of its scenes of fragmentary beauty, because it brought men closer together through their perversity and fear, because it enabled us to pretend that death could be a tender experience, and because it breached the long silence" (p. 27).

Much of the appeal of the "Bang, You're Dead" game is its simplicity. Like Gary and Myna's verbal play in the library, it harkens back to a less complicated time, here the simplicity of childhood. The most prominent example of the play-attitude in *End Zone* combines both the simplicity of "Bang, You're Dead" with the primitivism of the library scene. Central to the novel is the football game that is played in a blizzard. If sport is the closest we may come to order in an essentially chaotic world, then the snow football game is surely the most elemental form of sport.

The emphasis in the game is on play itself, not on winning or losing or execution. "The idea was to keep playing, keep moving, get it going again." The game begins as touch football, "five on a side, no contact except for brush blocks and tagging the ballcarrier" (p. 158). Through a series of rule changes the game is transformed into its most basic, elemental form. At the same time, all protections from the blizzarding snowfall are eliminated. First, the wearing of gloves is outlawed; next, the placing of hands under armpits between plays is outlawed. Then huddles are outlawed and each offensive play must be announced aloud. Thus, the defense knows what play is coming and the element of strategy is eliminated. "We were getting extremely basic, moving into elemental realms, seeking harmony with the weather and the earth" (p. 159). Soon passes and reverses are also outlawed. Tackling replaces tagging. Finally, end runs are banned. The game is thus reduced to its absolute most essential movement—straight-ahead running, blocking, and tackling. It becomes the head-to-head collision of bodies in deep snow with minimal visibility. The cold becomes so painful that "it hurt more than the blocking and tackling" (p. 161). The game grows from 10 to 14 players. No one complains about any of the rules: "We kept playing, we kept hitting, and we were comforted by the noise and brunt of our bodies in contact, by the simple physical warmth generated through violent action, by the sight of each other, the torn clothing, the bruises and scratches, the wildness of all fourteen, numb, purple, coughing, white heads solemn in the healing snow" (p. 161).

We begin to see that the snow football game, although it uses many of the outward forms of football, is a very different form of play from the football played by the Dallas professional team in *North Dallas Forty* or the Logos College team in *End Zone*. Unlike the game described at the beginning of this chapter, the snow football game is not played against the clock. It is not in any way limited by time and so it bears little resemblance to the "modern" game previously described as sharing in our current penchant for disaster and sudden reversals. In fact, there is no mention at all in the description of the snow football game of scoring or winning or losing. The game is played with no equipment except the ball itself, and the reductive rule changes have made the strategic offensive and defensive systems so pervasive in *North Dallas Forty* obsolete.

If the violence and pain of the game description sound masochistic, one can only say that it is not violence or pain for their own sake, but for the sake of rules, which structure the game, and for the sake of the game itself. It is an elemental form of play, to be sure, but a play-form gleefully entered into. The game has nothing to do with winning and losing. It is played for the sake of playing, because the play-attitude is absolutely compelling: "The idea was to keep playing, keep moving, get it going again" (p. 158). Unlike the image of football in *North Dallas Forty*, the snow football game in *End Zone*, like the "Bang, You're Dead" game, is played for its own sake. Instead of being part of a larger, mechanical, inhumane vision of life, play is here an end in itself, an expression of human joy, freedom (even freedom from time), and order amidst the meaningless chaos of the "end zone." In *North Dallas Forty* the pain and violence of football were symptomatic only of the larger social violence of America. The violence of football is the price individual players must pay for the opportunity to be part of the largest vicarious spectacle in America. And in *End Zone* the regular season games are not very much different from the sphere of professional football. After the Centrex game the injury report sounds more like a casualty list. But in the snow football game the emphasis is definitely upon the visceral reality of direct experience enjoyed for its own sake, not as a means to another end. The game is the fulfillment of the promise Charlotte Caulder's ranch held for Phil Elliott.

Although the vision of *End Zone* is more apocalyptic than that of *North Dallas Forty*, there are cracks in the enveloping conformity of technology. The pervasive metaphor of the machine in *North Dallas Forty* reaches its intellectual limits in *End Zone* and begins to break down. It would probably be misleading to say that the reductive world of *End Zone* is transcended by play, but that world is certainly made more meaningful and orderly by using the play-attitude to return to a simpler, more ritualized, more gamelike existence. At the very best, during those occasional moments when Phil Elliott forgets his precarious situation with the Dallas team management and realizes the joy and freedom of catching a football, he is able to play at his work. We are never far from the overwhelming evidence that professional football is the source of many intense conflicts for men like Phil Elliott. The flashes of freedom that he enjoys on the field or that Billy Tully and Ernie Munger feel in the ring are real, but, unfortunately, insignificant. Using Neale's psychological definition of play, one would have to classify the sport of *Fat City* and *North Dallas Forty* as work, for it is all "motivated by the need to resolve inner conflict." It is conflict which provides the impetus for Tully's comeback, for Ernie Munger's turning professional, and for Phil Elliott's several kow-towings to management.[21]

In *End Zone* we see for the first time the possibility of truly playing at play itself. In the "Bang, You're Dead" game the individual's sense of harmony is so great that it comes dangerously close to autism. For example, we get the following game description from Gary Harkness:

I died well and for this reason was killed quite often. One afternoon, shot from behind, I staggered to the steps of the library and remained there, on my back, between the second and seventh step at the approximate middle of the stairway, for more than a few minutes. It was very relaxing despite the hardness of the steps. I felt the sun on my face. I tried to think of nothing. The longer I remained there, the more absurd it seemed to get up. My body became accustomed to the steps and the sun felt warmer. I was completely relaxed. [Pp. 26-27.]

It is important to note in this description that the individual's aesthetic response to a game situation brings him into harmony not only with himself and others, but his natural environment as well. This seems all the more astounding when we consider that the environment here is only partially natural. We begin to wonder if Gary is in danger of not getting up at all. Robert E. Neale warns us that when harmony is total "there is complete absence of concern for survival."[22] Some conflict is therefore necessary to make play truly meaningful and to provide the impetus for survival.[23]

Along with the harmony of the player we find this measure of conflict in the snow football game. Here the natural environment is antagonistic and yet the players are "moving into elemental realms, seeking harmony with the weather and the earth" (p. 159). There is a deliberate attempt to force the pain of freezing snow on the players by making rules which prohibit protection from the elements. There is also a measure of violence among the players themselves, but here again the conflict is just enough to "allow that survival which can be transformed into the state of play."[24] Unlike the West Centrex contest, the violence of the snow football game is not an end in itself, but only part of the player's fascination with the game. Through the various games and rituals in *End Zone* there is, for the first time, the possibility of full human play. In every case the play-attitude is dependent upon a turning backward from the technological, mechanistic vision of the novel. The "order" of the machine age will either disintegrate in the apocalypse of uncontrolled nuclear war or become the meaningless geometry of an ascetic world of objects, epitomized by Taft Robinson's room. Gary apparently accepts the triumph of this sterile world, for after his last visit to Taft's room he loses his will to live. The ending of the novel is not very satisfying both because it fails to explain Gary's sucide attempt, and also because, ironically, he is saved by the very technology he would escape from. But the important thing is that we have had several strong glimpses of the power of the play impulse. It *is* possible to make the world more compelling, more meaningful, more orderly through play, and the way to achieve the play-attitude, as we have seen, is to go backward. The vision of *End Zone* is thus the vision of the brink. The choice the novel poses is the potential holocaust and chaos of a future with uncontrollable nuclear war, empty routines, and a meaningless language versus a return to a more primitive past where human activity is governed by rules, where sport is the product of harmony rather than conflict, and where the play-attitude may restore the expressive and poetic functions of language.

CHAPTER FIVE

"ONE ON ONE"

Zen and the Art of Basketball

The metaphorical texture and significance of sport are rendered with as much sensitivity and accuracy in Lawrence Shainberg's *One on One* as in any recent American novel. In its attempt to break from the muscular, naturalistic tradition in American sports fiction, Shainberg's novel ranks with Coover's *Universal Baseball Association* and Delillo's *End Zone* as one of the best introspective sports novels, and certainly the best basketball novel, of our time.

In *One on One* there is no apparent improvement in the condition of modern life as it is articulated in *End Zone*. The setting simply shifts from the barren Texas plains to New York City. Nuclear holocaust is no longer imminent, as it was in *End Zone*, but insistent casualty reports from Vietnam inform us that Shainberg's America is very similar to Gent's. Still, the difference in technique and vision marked by *End Zone* is large. The most striking clue to that difference between *One on One* and the other novels in this study is that in *One on One*, for the first time, there is a clear subordination of the conventional reliance upon plot as well as the realistic details which enhance plot. *Fat City* and *North Dallas Forty* are both characterized by a grim, visceral realism which is antagonistic to play. In *End Zone* the partial recovery of play coincides with a more fantastic, metaphorical concern with spontaneous games. The images of impending disaster give rise to lyrical moments of introspection almost completely absent in the first two novels. But there is still a realistic superstructure in *End Zone* which shapes and gives meaning to the events of the novel; the linear description of the season of a college football team focuses our attention. And it is significant that the three most important examples of the play-attitude in the novel take place before or after, not during, the season. Play is virtually absent from Logos College football. The season emphasizes conformity rather than ritual, obedience rather than freedom, and stultification rather than creativity.

One on One marks a significant break away from the realistic detail and linear structure in each of the previous novels. There is only the barest outline of "real" events in the novel; the realism of this book is psychological, and almost all the action is internalized as the fragmented experience of Elwood Baskin, a six-foot-nine-inch Jewish basketball player from Mississippi, on the day of his first varsity game for New York University. *One on One* shares with novels like *End Zone* a concern for the disintegration of modern life, but it is also like *The Universal Baseball Association* in that if focuses on individual fragmentation rather than cultural cataclysm. At the center of the novel is radical alienation, a vision of true atomism. The novel is thus a giant internalized landscape of a single mind creating, fantasizing, hallucinating, and commenting on itself. The emphasis on an external reality which focuses our attention upon significant action has been almost entirely replaced by self-consciousness.

The image of "one on one" in basketball jargon is equivocal. It frequently suggests a lack of cohesion, a breakdown in team play in favor of individual, even selfish, dis-play.[1] In this sense "one on one" is an appropriate metaphor for the chaos of Elwood's mind as well as the larger social psychosis of the world in which he lives. In addition to connotations of disharmony, however, "one on one" also describes the process of isolating a single offensive and defensive player against each other. Under those conditions each player must freelance his movements, and the result is often the most exciting and creative maneuvering and body control in the game. One-on-one situations are often extraordinary examples of playful sport in which the most essential characteristics of play—joy, freedom, and creativity—are epitomized.

The dual meanings of the "one on one" metaphor focus and shape the basic tension in the novel and lead to its resolution. Shainberg thus elaborates, through basketball, both the manic rage for control and order of the isolated individual trapped in his own self-consciousness, as well as the more transcendent values of play which, ultimately, are triumphant in this novel. Self-consciousness may be the trap from which Elwood must free himself, but it is also the means by which the world may be internalized and transcended. The real protagonist of *One on One* is not

Elwood so much as his mind, which brings together and re-creates all those people who are important to him. That phantasmagoria of chaotic relationships is surely too painful and proceeds from too much hostility to be playful. But self-consciousness is only an intermediate step to liberation for Elwood. There is another dimension to our experience of Elwood's mind which is altogether different from his personal relationships. While the world inside his head rages on as absurdly as ever, Elwood intermittently meditates on the aesthetics of basketball. There is a constant association in *One on One* of basketball with Eastern mysticism, with a movement out of the self-conscious ego toward liberation. Elwood's ruminations on basketball are poetic moments which elaborate the game as a metaphor for art, for the dance, and for all the transforming values associated with play.

The vision of most recent sports fiction includes an obsession with order, an obsession, often expressed by stultifying or overly abstract language, which seeks to control the numerous forms of social chaos. In books like *Fat City*, *End Zone*, *One on One*, and *The Universal Baseball Association* the rage for order often becomes so limiting and narrow as to be, paradoxically, more dangerous than the disorder it seeks to stay. In *End Zone*, for example, the monkish orderliness of Taft Robinson's room is, finally, sterile. The epigraphs to *One on One* herald the novel's central concern with order. This one, from Samuel Beckett's *Endgame*, might just as easily have been spoken by Taft Robinson in describing his room: "I love order. It's my dream. A world where all would be silent and still and each thing in its last place, under the last dust." Almost everyone in *One on One* has an alarming concern for order, control, or repetition. Herman Baskin eats exactly the same lunch each day and almost has a breakdown when the sandwich shop has the wrong kind of bread. He also compartmentalizes life into one-dimensional poses which are represented by an absurd series of gurus, culminating in Ernest Horton, the psychiatrist who is more compulsive than his patients. Minnie Baskin is obsessed with neatness and cleanliness, and has never set foot out of Moony, Mississippi, in spite of the fact that she, like her husband, is a multimillionaire. Indeed, the image of two Jewish millionaires in a small town in Mississippi with a 6'9" all-American basketball player son is reminiscent of the grotesqueries of black humor in the early sixties, and suggests one of the sources of the manic desire for control at any cost.

According to Horton, Elwood's size is one of the sources of his problem: "And size, yes of course: Size to some extent is the reason for it all. When a man is so huge, so powerful, so feared by those around him, he is terrified of the pain he might inflict if he were to lose control" (p. 31).[2] And when Elwood does lose control he almost kills Horton. Yet the fight with Horton is clearly therapeutic for Elwood. By punching Horton instead of talking to him, Elwood seeks to literally vanquish one of the voices in his head. The scene thus reinforces the idea that the desire for control, however understandable, is itself disastrous.

Although everyone in this novel is compulsive in one way or another, no one is quite so obsessed with order, restraint, and decorum as Ernest Horton. Just as the novel is a giant parody of psychoanalysis, so is Horton a marvellous perversion of all the worst aspects of psychotherapists. The rigid organization of his life is symptomatic of his personality:

> He had a peculiar way of answering the phone when he was working. . . . Usually, he cut it short, telling you to call back between one-fifteen and two-twenty, his lunch hour, or between seven-twenty when he finished his last patient, and eight-fifteen, when he sat down to work on his book. . . . He worked those hours for twelve weeks straight, then took three weeks' vacation. A month before his vacations began, he sent a locker full of books to the hotel where he'd be staying. He had been doing this, all of it, for eighteen years. Four nights a week he worked on whatever book he was writing, one on articles for psychoanalytic journals, one in teaching . . . , and one in relaxation—Friday night, when . . . he tried as best he could to "empty his mind." [P. 63.]

He is equally neurotic about the order and cleanliness of his desk. When Horton agrees to see Elwood during his lunch hour, it is the first time in eighteen years that the analyst has altered his schedule. After Elwood beats him up, the first thing Horton does is to reestablish the order on his desk: "Slouching in his chair, he rearranged his desk: straightened his pile of notebooks, moved the Buddha two inches to the left, the African sculpture two inches to the right, emptied the ashtray, which was already empty" (p. 124).

The item on Horton's desk which tells us most about him is his copy of *Roget's Thesaurus*. For Horton, as for so many characters in *End Zone*, language is a special source of control. As it becomes increasingly abstract and jargony, language also becomes evasive, self-serving, and sterile. In one of his scholarly monographs Horton talks about the "tendency toward too-great abstractionism" as a bar to "creative, inspired modes of thought and being" (p. 143). And yet as that sentence, even the word "abstractionism," shows, he is the character most to blame for a deadening language which is alienating, uninspired, calculated, and, typically, unintelligible. As a parodist of social science jargon Horton has few equals:

That the existential-ontological is in effect an addendum, a profoundation, and a clearly defined extension of psychiatry, is to be perceived in historical perspective. The ontogenic drive encounters in experience numerous impediments which affect and involve the existential-ontological orientation and potentiality of the self-encumbered individual. [P. 137.]

Even a brief passage on "love" does not reify that elusive term, and only makes it more abstract: "Love as a mode of cognition is concerned with truth, with meaning, and with the unhindered unfolding of the ontogenic thrust" (p. 137). As Thelma Lemming (whose name is a tipoff as to her credibility, and who, incidentally, has underlined the above words) says, "It's a difficult concept to articulate" (p. 137).

In Elwood's mind or in his own office, Horton is never seen without his notebook. Words are Horton's strength, although he uses them to disengage himself from direct experience. He is a voyeur, a parasite, feeding on the fantasies of others, but without any fantasies of his own. Significantly, when Elwood throws Horton across his own office and bloodies his face, Horton talks about that frightening event as *"real experience."* Horton has been genuinely ruffled; his order has been momentarily disrupted. And so he automatically resorts to his greatest strength and begins to chatter, "yes, maybe this was good for me . . . maybe we're too cloistered, we analysts . . . maybe we ought to have more experiences like this . . . more *real* experience. . . . Some fact to go with our philosophy!" (p. 124). More importantly, Horton's theorizing about his visceral experience robs his sentiment of any truth it may have had.

Horton's entire sense of reality—which he describes in his endless monographs—is based exclusively upon vicarious rather than direct experience. He even wants to watch Elwood play basketball so that he can write an article about him, get him down on paper once and for all. Horton is thus the most unplayful character in the novel. In Robert E. Neale's psychological definition of play, Horton epitomizes the work self: "The profane or work self is dedicated to the goal of minimizing risk and fostering routine. Its basic reaction to new experience is anxiety, for the breaking up of rigidity appears as chaos to the individual."[3] The sterility of Horton's routines cannot tolerate the intrusion of any direct experience, of any potentially liberating feeling, of any play. And so when Herman and Minnie Baskin begin to swear at each other (their own and personal gameness), expressing both love and hate with their profanity—any emotion will do—Horton becomes expendable. The beginning of love in Moony (in Elwood's head) is the end of Horton's control. In fact the tension between the deadening weight of Horton's own personality and rigid methodology and the freedom he seeks to give his patients is at least as schizophrenic as Elwood's fantasies.

As in *End Zone,* language in *One on One* is perverted from a potentially expressive and playful medium to an empty, chaotic, and meaningless one. Language has ceased altogether to be referential and has become purely reflexive, self-contained, in a word, mad. Although Horton's compulsive organization and empty classifications make him the major enemy of play in this novel, he is by no means the only one.

It would be reasonable enough if Lavelli, Elwood's basketball coach at New York University, sounded like most coaches and numbed us with his clichés, but for Elwood he is more than just a simple-minded user of sports jargon. At the team lunch Lavelli begins outlining the strategy for the night game against Duke: "He was suddenly another Horton in my mind, another word-factory, I mean, whose main job in life was to weigh me down with his ideas" (p. 152). While Elwood wants to talk about the instinct and magic of basketball, Lavelli has reduced the game to a series of diagrams: " 'Angles!' he cried. 'Defense is nothing but angles! He takes his step—boom!—you take yours. Who's got the angle? That's the question!' " (p. 153). The jargon here is highly reminiscent of the abstractions in *End Zone* ("History is the angle at which realities meet" or "Football is . . . an interlocking of a number of systems"). I am not implying that Delillo was influenced by Shainberg, or even that he read *One on One*, but it is interesting that in their respective concerns for the tension between the reductivism of a decaying language and the liberation of play both writers have established the same vocabulary and used much of the same rhetoric. Coincidence or not, Lavelli's vocabulary has the same implications as the language most typically used in *End Zone*—paralysis and sterility. There is not much difference between the stultifying order of Taft Robinson's room and Lavelli's diagrams—or Horton's rigid organization. "If things happened on the court the way coaches diagram them, every game would come to a standstill: a perfect offense and a perfect defense add up to a state of paralysis. . . . It was the second time that day that Lavelli had reminded me of Horton; because that's the way I saw most of Horton's theories" (p. 155).

In addition to Horton and Lavelli, the "word-factories" in this novel include Michael Malbin, a grotesque parody of a public relations expert. He is *End Zone*'s Wally Pippich without any of Pippich's playfulness. Michael considers himself Elwood's "personal historian" and, like Horton, takes notes on everything he says or does. Michael's notes cover every observable facet of Elwood's life from his fetish for Mars bars to the Ring Ding wrappers which litter his room. He picks up "detail like a vacuum cleaner" and then catalogs his information on individual cards, once again compartmentalizing Elwood's life.

Elwood is merely a pawn through whom others accomplish their sterile re-creation and reordering of the world. For Michael, Elwood is the ultimate public relations challenge. Where Pippich, who did at least have imagination, used only the scantiest information to create an image (albeit a false one), Michael's notecards are an absurd rejection of the public's demand for information. Once Elwood feels himself being re-created for public consumption his dissociation seems natural: "When he looked at me, he didn't see me, but 'Elwood Baskin,' the product he was making and selling to the world. . . . The way he saw it, I think, he was an artist and I was his creation. Without him I didn't exist at all" (pp. 54-55).

Such plot as there is in *One on One* includes an example of one of Michael's public relations triumphs: Elwood's taped television interview with Chuck Lewis. Any possible integrity that public language may have once had is undercut during the interview. Not only are the questions insipid, but Lewis does not even allow Elwood to answer them truthfully. The "truth" here for Elwood's "serious fans" demands that he lie about his nervousness. The second part of the interview, in which Elwood's answers are, if anything, even more inane, and which for depth, color, and originality might satisfy the curiosity of a daffodil, elicits from Lewis the response, " 'Now we're getting somewhere' " (p. 73). Lewis and his cronies refuse to acknowledge one of the novel's central perceptions: that people and environments are constantly changing. Rather than admit the essential instability of the world, Lewis attempts to fix Elwood in time and space, to encapsulate him in prescribed answers to moronic questions. Lewis defies the fragmentation and flux of the world which is at the heart of *One on One*, and so the interview becomes still another compulsive form of attempted control.

Given the neuroticism of every major character in the novel, is it even reasonable to search for "normality" in this world? The confusion between reality and fantasy is at the heart of *One on One*, and everything in the novel—structure, technique, character, theme—contributes to the blurring and blending of the two. Horton says at one point, "In the inner world of mental illness, illusion and reality are finally one" (p. 184). For once Horton is right, but I would argue that his analysis holds for both Elwood's inner reality and for the external world as well. The point at which Jeannie finally realizes the magnitude of Elwood's sickness is precisely the point at which he begins to feel better. In order to get a sense of his own reality Elwood looks at pictures of himself in the newspaper. And Horton, the one character who has the most compulsive and regimented life, is charged with the task of liberating others. While the convergence of reality and fantasy in the external world is seen as schizophrenic, internally it may be liberating. The caution with which one should approach Elwood's schizophrenia is articulated by Horton in one of his more Laingian moments: "Insanity, you know, is often a path to freedom. Who are we to save him from it?" (p. 32).

Horton would do well to take his own advice. For while everyone attributes Elwood's "illness" to basketball, Elwood himself attributes it to Horton. Basketball is merely the means by which he got to Horton's office in the first place. Whatever freedom is possible in *One on One* has nothing to do with psychotherapy. There *are* mystical moments of transcendence here, but they are always associated with basketball, with play, or with art. Basketball, as an aesthetic experience, or associated with Chud's sculpture, is play which transcends the chaos, pettiness, and absurdity of the urban wasteland. Significantly, basketball is that part of the world which Elwood successfully internalizes. Elwood himself never actually plays basketball in the present time of the novel, and we are witness to only one playground game.

Even on the playground, the only play which remains a part of the description of external reality, basketball is fully realized play, akin, for example, to the separated play-world of Coover's *Universal Baseball Association* or the snow football game in *End Zone*. The playground which Elwood passes with Michael on his way to the interview is a small run-down park on the outskirts of Greenwich Village, which in fact is one of New York City's more prestigious courts, and Shainberg has captured the superficial dreariness of the place perfectly. One should not be fooled, however, as to the importance of what takes place on the court. Huizinga's description of play is to the point: "All play moves and has its being within a play-ground marked off beforehand either materially or ideally, deliberated or as a matter of course. Just as there is no formal difference between play and ritual, so the 'consecrated spot' cannot be formally distinguished from the play-ground."[4] The basketball court, like all playgrounds, is a sacred place in the midst of a profane world—in *One on One* there is "too much traffic noise to hear the sound of the ball"—within which, as Huizinga says, "special rules obtain."[5]

The emphasis in Shainberg's description of playground basketball is strikingly similar to Delillo's account of the snow football game in *End Zone*. In *End Zone*, the game was described this way: "The idea was to keep playing, keep moving, get it going again" (p. 158). The game was violent, primal, but there was no complaining, little chatter, and no score was kept. It was play for its own sake. In *One on One* the game is again its own reward: "They were bouncing off the fence, sliding on the concrete, throwing knees and elbows like clubs. No laughter, no talk, no teamwork. Unlike college and professional players, they took the game down to its most essential problem: put the ball in the basket as quickly and as often as the other team allowed. *Playground basketball*. What you played for here wasn't fame, or money, or headlines, or trophies, but 'winners'— the right to go on playing. One loss and you might sit out for the rest of the day" (p. 56). Keeping score is not an end in itself but a way of determining who continues to play. This is essential, compelling play, play for its own sake: "They would go on like this all day, all winter, all spring, all summer, as long as there was light and the court was dry. If you got a good combination and kept on winning, you could play for ten hours a day. . . . That was the only reward here, but it was enough. You'd never see anyone stop for being tired" (p. 57).

There are some fifty spectators to this pickup game, an extraordinary number considering that the location of the game is a neighborhood park. But the impact of the game, especially in an urban environment, is considerable and has been duly noted by social scientists. In Pete Axthelm's phrase, basketball is "the city game." It requires neither the number of players nor the extensive equipment of baseball and football. And for grace, movement, and excitement basketball is the equal of any sport. The order that Horton seeks to preserve in his office may be found much more meaningfully in the nearest pickup basketball game where "a classic play is frozen in the minds of those who see it—a moment of order and achievement in a turbulent, frustrating existence."[6]

Beyond the one example of playground ball, all the references to basketball in *One on One* are introspective. There are meditations on the essence of the sport, fantasies of what the game against Duke will be like, and artistic representations of basketball in the form of Chud's sculpture. Each of these play-forms frees both Elwood and the game from the manic connotations of the title metaphor and makes available the full, mature play-attitude. Through the imaginative re-creation of sport, play becomes a transcendent reality in *One on One*. In naturalistic sports novels like *North Dallas Forty* and *Fat City* play exists only as a grim illusion because the body is a mere instrument or tool. Shainberg's vision, however, includes the awareness that for play to become transforming the movements of the game and the intuitions behind them must be inseparable.

The pivotal moment in Elwood's life thus comes before the action of the novel, when he saw Lucius McCarver's jump shot on television and first realized the possibility of instinctive play in basketball: "For the first time in the history of the game, the shot and the impulse to shoot were almost simultaneous. . . . You couldn't plan anymore or figure what to do. You had to make the move and let the idea wait for later" (p. 20). The jump shot becomes the focal point of Elwood's life. He practices endlessly to perfect it, and then "suddenly it was all there, working together and of its own accord, separate from my mind or anything I'd learned about it" (p. 21). The shot, which Elwood sees as a "gift," is transforming: "There was almost no relationship between the person I was before the jump shot and the person I was after" (p. 21).

Elwood's entire existence becomes caught up in the game, so much so that his father is worried that there is "nothing else in the world but the game." That last phrase might just as easily describe the separated, mythic play-world of Coover's final chapter of *The Universal Baseball Association*. Herman Baskin is obviously one of those dichotomists who, by social conditioning, divide the world into too-rigid dualisms such as game/reality or play/life. However, there is nothing in Herman's warning which is at all incompatible with recent play theory, most of which discusses games and play as the most comprehensive metaphors for human activity. Kostas Axelos goes so far as to use "game" as a metaphor for "planetary thought": " 'Game' is not a slogan. After you have discovered it, it is no great exploit to find it; the difficulty will be henceforth to forget it. In it everything is constructed and destroyed. Being and non-being, nature, God and man would be its masks. . . ."[7] The problem is then not whether there should be anything in the world besides the game, but to what extent the game, because of its potential for play, may help us recover the joy, freedom, and creativity of the play-attitude.

Elwood's descriptions of "Touch" and "Defense" make it clear that basketball makes available a transcendent experience completely denied in the deadening world outside the game. Touch is an element of the game which defies rational explanation:

> If you have touch, the ball is part of your hands. You shoot it, dribble it, pass it, but it never leaves your hands. . . . The biggest part of touch is feeling—the feeling of *rightness*, almost of magic when you touch the ball and start to shoot it. . . . Before the ball leaves your hands you know the shot is good. You don't have to watch. The ball will travel through an arc maybe forty feet long and land perfectly in the center of a hoop twenty-four inches in diameter and you *know*. Not because you've decided somewhere in your mind to shoot so hard, so high, and give the ball just so much spin, but because suddenly you and the ball and the hoop are *together*, all of one piece, and it is impossible to miss. [P. 38.]

Elwood has captured the essence of the game here, but that essence defies the rules of logic. The description of touch transports the reader into the mystical heart of basketball. The "magic" of touch is ultimately inexpressible because it is sacred. Even Horton, the novel's most unplayful character, realizes that the old dualisms won't work: "The word 'game' has always had a negative connotation in our culture. Play, like humor, is a sacred activity, but the Judeo-Christian ethic has always condemned it as childish" (p. 166). In his book on the theology of play, David Miller makes the same point: "In the Genesis account, as in other religions' accounts of creation, the fall from a paradisiacal bliss of primal play is marked and marred by a new burden of labor and a bondage to a sense of life as being serious. . . . Originally there was pure unequivocal play. . . . Serious activity may be viewed as play; play is serious. There is no necessary dichotomy."[8]

Shainberg is obviously more interested in the potential for play in Eastern philosophy than in the Judeo-Christian tradition. The allusions to Lao Tzu and Herrigel's *Zen in the Art of Archery* reinforce basketball's affinities with mystical experience. The tension between the two traditions is pointed up by Elwood's argument with Coach Lavelli over defensive strategy. Lavelli's conception of defense is mechanical, prescriptive, and unimaginative. It has no affinity whatsoever with play, is only a matter of "angles." (The abstract, mathematical jargon is significant, too.) Like so many other characters in recent sports fiction, Lavelli is a pragmatist who wants to manipulate the potential play experience for his own profane ends.[9] His reaction to the game is as profane as Horton's approach to therapy. Both men minimize risk by fostering routine.[10]

Radically different from Lavelli's inartistic approach to defense is Elwood's notion of play which is instinctive. For example, Elwood explains how he will defense Reeves: "Instinct, that's how! When he moves, I move with him! No thinking . . . I do it automatically . . . because I'm not just playing him, see, I'm inside his head . . . ! Defense is instinct, and instinct . . . is magic!" (pp. 153-54). Where Lavelli's defensive strategy is reductive, Elwood's is mystical. Lavelli would formulize the game, while Elwood's play transcends the possibility of unimaginative calculation. Elwood's play coincides with Howard Slusher's existential analysis of sport which epitomizes the play-attitude: "Athletes, in general . . . at some point in time, come to realize that there is something beyond *all* that is mortal, *all* that is comprehensible by the human mind. Within the movement of the athlete a wonderful mystery of life is present, a mystical experience that is too close to the religious to call it anything else."[11]

Elwood's emphasis on vitality and instinct is also crucial to Eugen Fink's ontological analysis of play. For Fink, "The mode of play is that of spontaneous act, of vital impulse. Play is, as it were, existence centered in itself."[12] The movement of both Fink's philosophy and Shainberg's fiction is toward a conception of play which shatters once and for all the limiting and rigid dichotomy between play and reality. Shainberg is consciously pushing us toward the understanding that full play must be so compelling as to be "existence centered in itself": "What you know once you're into the game . . . is that there is almost no work involved in playing. It's like finding the central current in a river and letting it carry you downstream. Once you're inside the game, once you give up your fear, it is really harder not to play than play: the only thing you have to do is let it happen" (p. 62). The "fear" is clearly the risk of "adventure" that Robert E. Neale so poignantly describes, the same fear which makes the play experience inaccessible to pragmatists like Billy Tully and Ernie Munger in *Fat City*, Lou Engel in *The Universal Baseball Association*, or Seth Maxwell in *North Dallas Forty*. Once again there is the mystical allusion to "the river," and again Elwood's conception of the game comes remarkably close to Fink's play theory: "Each plaything represents the totality of objects: play is always a confrontation with Being. In the plaything the whole is concentrated in a single object. Each game is an attempt at existence, a vital experiment that encounters in the plaything the essence of unyielding reality."[13]

The game is so real, so compelling, so essential an attempt at existence, that it becomes the substance of the novel's ultimate vision—Chud's basketball sculpture. It is essential to make a distinction between Chud's original conception of the sculpture and Elwood's horrifying fantasy of it. In Elwood's fantasy he becomes trapped inside his plaster mold and thus is consigned to die there. On this level the sculpture and the fantastic murder trial Elwood imagines represent death and sterility. But the initial vision of the sculpture is obviously interesting enough to compel Elwood's attention—focus his fantasies, so to speak. And the reason why Elwood finds the idea of the sculpture so fascinating is that it combines basketball and art in a single transcendent vision and thus supports all the liberating values he associates with the game.

By elevating sport to the level of art, Shainberg challenges the reader to evaluate Elwood's vision of basketball as a transcendent reality. He poses the spectacle of Chud's sculpture as an alternative to the sterility of Horton and Michael Malbin. The notion that playful sport has an aesthetic dimension is not new to careful observers of play and sport. In fact, the comparison between sport and art is central to much recent writing about sport. Even René Maheu, who suggested that sport gives rise to few significant works of culture, says that "sport is a creator of beauty. In the action and rhythm which testify to mastery and time, sport becomes akin to the arts which create beauty. No athlete can accomplish a genuine feat without such perfect control . . . that his movements and the rhythm of their timing are not to be differentiated from the finest ballet. . . ."[14] Howard Slusher is willing to push the comparison even further. He sees sport as not only "real" experience, but, like Shainberg, a dynamic synthesis of several kinds of experience which may well result in full, mature play.[15]

Because of its grace, constant movement, and intricate patterns, basketball seems an especially good choice for the elevation Shainberg has chosen for sport. Former NBA star Bill Bradley has described his teammate, Walt Frazier, using the analogy of basketball and dance: "He plays with smooth and effortless grace, as if he were a dancer revealing the beauty of a body in movement."[16] In a broader context Pete Axthelm has also described basketball with the metaphor of the dance: ". . . its simple motions swirl into intricate patterns, its variations become almost endless, its brief soaring moments merge into a fascinating dance."[17] The metaphor is particularly appropriate because both the game and the dance make possible, in a moment in time, the unity of art and artist. The emphasis in Chud's conception of the sculpture is to capture the game in process, "In action, dig? To catch the rhythm, the tension, the drama of the game!" (p. 92). The unity of movement and stasis is as essential to the vision of Chud's work as it is to Yeats's dancer and dance, Keats's "still unravished bride of quietness," even Eliot's "still point of the turning world."

Chud's claim that "There's been nothing like it in the entire history of art" (p. 90) is pure egocentricity. The use of mundane objects in modern sculpture is fairly common, particularly in the work of George Segal. However, Segal and others use these objects to depict stasis, paralysis, and lethargy in their works. Chud *is* different in that he seeks to use the literal representation of sport as an imaginative re-creation of transcendent experience. The sculpture depicts Elwood perpetually in the process of shooting, never releasing the ball but also never returning to a static position on the court. The instant in time which the sculpture captures, like Keats's frieze, is eternally in the process of becoming and thus transcends temporality. The game, like all aesthetic experiences, makes available to the player a quintessential element of full play— liberation from the "futurism" and goal-oriented anticipation of modern life. "In the autonomy of play action there appears a possibility of human timelessness in time. Time is then experienced, not as a precipitate rush of successive moments, but rather as the one full moment that is, so to speak, a glimpse of eternity."[18]

Basketball, through its association with instinctiveness, joy, creative freedom, and magic is a manifestation of sport as sacred play. The imaginative re-creation of the game as art and mystical experience makes possible the recovery of playful values in a rigid and deadening environment. While the vision of Chud's sculpture comes relatively early in the novel, Elwood continues his meditation on the game throughout the day. The liberation of the game is constantly posed as an alternative to the voices in his head.

The movement of the entire novel may be seen as Elwood's triumph over the egocentric, sterile voices which seek to control him. While the reader is left with a strong feeling of assurance that Elwood will play brilliantly in his college debut, perhaps we cannot get the actual game description because Elwood's victory is ultimately a triumph over language. His final expansive smile symbolizes his transcendence of stultifying words. As he told Lavelli at the team lunch, "What we're looking for is peace and joy. And magic. Magic most of all!" (p. 152). Unlike *End Zone*, where the mechanical uses of language are only partially redeemed by the expressive language play in the library, in *One on One* Shainberg seems to be arguing that, since language is sterile, play is only possible in some imaginative realm beyond words. Elwood's final smile is dynamic, and is an appropriate image for the play he is about to engage in, but the tension between words and play can never be finally resolved in a novel which must use language to describe that very tension.

The conclusion of the novel is a confirmation of the measure of freedom Elwood has attained in the course of his day. His fantasy about Chud's sculpture, in which he is trapped inside the plaster cast, is a special strategy that he invents to kill himself symbolically and thus free himself from Horton's interminable analysis.[19] What Minnie Baskin fears is her son's death is merely the death of the old schizoid Elwood who has been plagued by psychoanalysis. Our final glimpse of Elwood is far more optimistic than last glances at the protagonists of other recent sports novels. Instead of, say, Gary Harkness's attempted suicide in *End Zone*, Elwood's parting image is radiant. The reader leaves him, appropriately, as he steps onto the court for his first college basketball game. However temporary Elwood's triumph may be, for the moment at least he is free of the voices which plagued him and ready to embark on the creative adventure of full, human play.

CHAPTER SIX

"THE UNIVERSAL BASEBALL ASSOCIATION"

Play as Personalized Myth

Robert Coover's *The Universal Baseball Association, Inc.–J. Henry Waugh, Proprietor* is the most far-reaching exploration of play in this study. Like these other novels, Coover's admits a tension between the literal representation of modern America and the imaginative re-creation of sport and play. That tension is now manifested, however, in a way directly opposed to the naturalistic focus of *Fat City*. Here the material world is almost entirely subsumed by the imaginative world of play. In *Fat City* and in *North Dallas Forty* as well, the naturalistic technique reveals a deep hostility between the world of sport and the possibility of playful adventure. In *End Zone* play is partially recovered, but only insofar as individuals, free of social or organizational pressures, can seize the impulse of a moment and respond to it spontaneously. There is nothing in the description of actual college football which is playful. Even in *One on One*, where basketball is internalized as mystical experience, the transcendent value of sport is at least balanced by the hostile and worklike rage for control in the world outside the game. That manic search for order which, thus far, has always been part of the literal world, is replaced in *The Universal Baseball Association* by a natural system of rules which becomes an intrinsic part of the play-world itself. Henry Waugh's game provides its own order, an order so radically self-contained that it creates its own course and meaning, entirely cut off from such

* The material in this chapter originally appeared, in slightly different form, in *Modern Fiction Studies*, Copyright © 1978 by Purdue Research Foundation, West Lafayette, Indiana, U.S.A.

established mythic traditions as are employed in Malamud's *The Natural* and Roth's *The Great American Novel*. The triviality of the work sphere is emphasized in *The Universal Baseball Association* not only, as in the other four novels, by its compulsiveness, but also, and for the first time, by the skimpiness of plot outside the game. Henry Waugh's baseball game is so fertile in metaphorical significance that there is virtually no activity in Henry's life upon which the game does not impinge. There is nothing the game cannot include. But the game is more than a metaphor, too; eventually, Henry's Association becomes the world. In *One on One*, play is defined over and against a dreary external reality, while in *The Universal Baseball Association* baseball provides the inspiration for the creation of an entire world.

Henry is the only character in any of the novels in this study who can bear the full weight of Eugen Fink's ontological definition of play: "The player experiences himself as the lord of the products of his imagination—because it is virtually unlimited, play is an eminent manifestation of human freedom."[1] Fink's remarks point up the great distance between *Fat City* and *The Universal Baseball Association*. In *Fat City* there is no imagination, only manipulation on the part of the would-be players. In *North Dallas Forty*, *End Zone*, and *One on One* there is an increasing emphasis upon the imagination of the players, but that imagination is either overwhelmed *(North Dallas Forty)* or at least grossly disrupted *(One on One)* by an antagonistic emphasis upon control. In *The Universal Baseball Association* imagination is so truly protean that it becomes an end in itself. The final vision of the novel is of a complete play-world, personalized and separated as myth, art, and religion.

John Steinbeck once said of baseball that "There is no way to explain that baseball is not a sport or a game or a contest. It is a state of mind, and you can't learn it."[2] For Henry Waugh, and for Robert Coover playing with his protagonist, baseball surely has the force of an idea. It is an abstraction to be played with and explored as the focus of Henry's imaginative universe. Real baseball always bored Henry. What initially attracted him to the game were "the records, the statistics, the peculiar balances between individual and team, offense and defense, strategy and luck, accident and pattern, power and intelligence. And no other activity in the world had so precise and comprehensive a history, so specific an ethic, and at the same time, strange as it seemed, so much ultimate mystery" (p. 38).[3] Even the most traditional of game accoutrements, the playing board, has been eliminated. At one time Henry used "a mock-up of a ball park, but it only got in the way" (p. 131); instead, he uses the more abstract statistics and qualities described above to create the game as a product of his imagination.

The remarkable richness and vitality of Henry Waugh's Association mark it as a self-enclosed world. Indeed, the ascription "Universal Baseball Association" forewarns the reader that nothing as petty or parochial as "American" or "National" is intended. The Association has its own metaphysics and must be seen as the product of a godlike creative act. Henry's initials—J. H. W.—identify him with the Hebrew god Yahweh. He has created the eight teams in his Association, all the personnel of those teams, and the physical and biographical data of his players. The tiresome naturalistic world of Henry's accounting job is trivial beside his Association, but both worlds exist and exert some influence over Henry's being. The novel thus argues that play may establish a relative metaphysics. When Henry decides to return to work after the exhausting game in which Damon Rutherford is killed, we see his own confusion about which world is more real and vital as he buys a newspaper, "obeying some old impulse which, he realized, he'd nearly forgotten, the giving of the coin, the snapping up of the paper, taking the world to heart and mind, or some world anyway" (p. 96). This relativity is in keeping with Kostas Axelos' "Planetary Thought": "When speaking of the game of the world we should not forget that all the games we play and which involve us completely are always intra-world in the world and in time. Never do we find ourselves in the presence of the World and of Time, of the Game itself; our dependence is always situated inside their fragments."[4] *The Universal Baseball Association* confronts the reader with a vision of play and reality as radically interdependent. In addition to the figure of Henry Waugh, who plays with the actors in his game-world, the reader is never allowed to forget for long that Robert Coover is playing with Henry Waugh, with numbers, with language, and with myth. Even the players in the Association play baseball and act out rituals. The playfulness of the book thus exists on several levels simultaneously and shatters the idea that reality must be played out against a fixed and stable background.

One of the most important aspects of the game—and a sure sign of Coover's delight in playing games—is the naming of players. The inspiration for a player's name often comes from a sign Henry happens to see, but any words that happen to catch Henry's attention are played with, perhaps recombined, until the sound is right for a ballplayer's name. Henry's naming is a more formalized version of the language play in the library in *End Zone*. Once a rookie has a name, his actual accomplishments on the field begin to give the name a certain character, fill out its appropriateness, but the initial act is the creative one. Henry knows the weight of what he is about; the artistry of naming has consequences: "name a man and you make him what he is. Or something can go wrong. Lots of nicknames invented as a result of Rookie-year suprises. But the basic stuff is already there. In the name. Or rather: in the naming" (p. 40). Coover may be trying to show the consistency (or limitedness?) of Henry's imagination, or it may be sheer playful perversity on the author's part, but in fact almost every player in the Association has an Anglo/Irish name. The only obvious exceptions are some parodic names—including Yip Yick Ping, Bruiser Brusatti, and Agapito Bacigamupo—none of whom figures very prominently in the novel. Perhaps the best explanation is that since names form the emotional center of the game, Henry is wary of those which may be too eccentric. "Henry was always careful about names, for they were what gave the league its sense of fulfillment and failure, its emotion. The dice and charts and other paraphernalia were only the mechanics of the drama, not the drama itself. Names had to be chosen, therefore, that could bear the whole weight of perpetuity" (p. 39).

The last phrase gives some indication as to the scope of Henry's essentially historical imagination. Because of its long tradition as the national pastime, and because of the accessibility of its records and statistics, baseball is a fine metaphor for history, process, and order. It is history and continuity which most fascinate Henry, and that is why he has always been somewhat anxious about the gratuitousness of the Association's beginnings:

In spite of the almost excessive warmth he felt toward those first ballplayers, it always troubled him that their life histories were so unavailable to him: What had a great player already in his thirties been doing for the previous ten years? It was much better once a kind of continuity had been established, and when new players had taken over the league who had their whole careers still ahead of them. It was, in fact, when the last Year I player had retired that Henry felt the Association had come of age, and when, a couple of years ago, Barnaby North had died, he had felt an odd sense of relief: the touch with the deep past was now purely "historic," its ambiguity only natural. Luckily, all the first-year records had been broken. And soon there would be no more living veterans born before Year I. [Pp. 38-39.]

Once all of those first-year records have been broken, all the game's hallmarks are products of a historical continuum and can thus be explained with the same kind of logic that orders the playing of the game.

Briefly, the game is played by tossing three dice; the numbers determine what happens on the playing field. If certain combinations come up, reference must be made to a special "Stress Chart." And the very unlikely possibility of rolling 1-1-1 twice in a row necessitates the use of the "Extraordinary Occurrences Chart" where another roll can produce such extraordinary occurrences as a hitter killing a pitcher with a line drive or a batter being killed by a beanball. Every contingency has been accounted for; even the eventual demise of players is tabulated with the aid of Henry's actuarial tables. While Henry is the creator of his game, his power is limited by the rules and forms of the game itself. Henry's only real choice—at least initially—is whether or not to actuate the game by throwing the dice. Henry religiously transcribes the records and statistics of the Association, but the substance of the game is determined by the dice, "three ivory cubes, heedless of history yet makers of it" (p. 18).

There would appear to be a strong measure of dispassionate logic about all this; the game contains within itself an order which seems unshakeable. If Henry himself were a dispassionate god, the history which he records would be as mechanical as the tossing of the dice. But Henry is not at all detached. Those names he has created mean something to him. The historical relationships developed over many seasons transcend the mere statistical accounts of games recorded in the Book, the bible of the game world. The game world is so engaging that even a local bartender named Pete becomes the embodiment of Jake Bradley, a former Association great, and Henry cannot forbear referring to the place as "Jake's." When Henry's actuarial tables inform him that Jake Bradley has died, the reality of the play-world demands that Henry can no longer inhabit Pete's bar, since Pete *cum* Jake is dead. While the dice may be heedless of history, Henry is not. Even the Association's fielding statistics must be faithfully recorded, although they are dull and make few discriminations among ballplayers. Here again, Henry's commitment is to history as a source of order and continuity: "He had thought of giving them up altogether, they took a lot of time and didn't seem worth it, but there were all those fielding records already established, and what would they mean if they had no challengers?" (p. 44).

The novel opens, appropriately, as Damon Rutherford, a star rookie pitcher in the Association, is in the process of pitching a history-making perfect game. Damon also happens to be the son of Brock Rutherford, the central figure in the Association's first great era. From the outset one sees the dangerous involvement of the creator in the world of his game.

Henry *is* aware, at this point in the novel, that there is some difference between the game and external reality: Coover emphasizes that Henry is "sweating with relief and tension all at once, unable to sit, unable to think, *in* there, *with* them" (p. 9). But the game is surely the more compelling reality, so much so that when Henry wants to get a snack his impulse *must* coincide with the traditional seventh inning stretch which marks a break in the action of the game. And when in his mind's eye he sees the warm-up pitches for the next inning, Henry knows he must hurry back to the game with his food. We know that the game cannot continue until Henry throws the dice again, but Henry's sense of urgency indicates that the game has its own momentum, much the same kind of momentum that Elwood Baskin ascribed to the voices in his head.

Henry's engagement with his play-world, although dangerous, is not surprising. Robert E. Neale has aptly described the mature player in terms which closely fit Henry Waugh and his imaginative universe: "He does not alternately fight the world and escape from it as the secular woker does, nor does he usefully and abusively covenant with it as the magical worker does. Rather, the full adult adventurer is in communion with the world, demonstrating the love that is identical to that expressed by the gods in their creation of the world in the beginning."[5] Henry's communion with his Association is so complete that the game dominates all of his routine activities. Even some casual sex with a B-girl is only possible insofar as Henry can correlate the metaphors of sex with those of baseball and identify completely with his heroic creation of Damon Rutherford.

In one of the book's most dazzling examples of verbal playfulness, Coover makes all of the above images work together as Henry and Hettie have intercourse:

"Damon," she whispered, unbuckling his pants, pulling his shirt out. And "Damon," she sighed, stroking his back, unzipping his fly, sending his pants earthward with a rattle of buckles and coins. And "Damon!" she greeted, grabbing—and that girl, with one swing, he knew then, could bang a pitch clean out of the park. *"Play ball!"* cried the umpire. And the catcher, stripped of mask and guard, revealed as the pitcher Damon Rutherford, whipped the uniform off the first lady ballplayer in Association history, and then, helping and hindering all at once, pushing and pulling, they ran the bases, pounded into first, slid into second heels high, somersaulted over third, shot home standing up, then into the box once more, swing away, and run them all again, and "Damon!" she cried, and "Damon!" [Pp. 26-27].

The point of this marvellous passage seems to be that Henry is as much a part of his own game as his players, and furthermore, that both Henry and the Association are parts of a larger game being played by still another god figure—Robert Coover. The significance of that manipulation is brilliantly pointed up by Jacques Ehrmann's critique of the play theories of Huizinga and Caillois, who "erred principally in never doubting . . . that the player is the subject of play; in believing that, present in the game, at the center of play, they dominated it. They forgot that players may be played; that, as an object in the game, the player can be its stakes (*enjeu*) and its toy (*jouet*)."[6] The implication is that unless Henry realizes that he and the game are part of the same stakes, that both he and the game are subject *and* object of play, he is destined for a severe blow, which comes swiftly enough in the death of Damon Rutherford.

The game-world has always had the apparent means for dealing with death, but always in the abstract form of statistics; older, retired ball-players are "sorted out" of the Association on the basis of Henry's actuarial tables. But death in the impalpable form of mere statistics is an evasion. The death of Damon Rutherford marks the introduction of something new and significant into the game-world, and makes death, for the first time, a concrete reality. Henry is more deeply committed to Damon than any other player in the Association and that personal involvement, which as I have already noted even manifests itself in Henry's sexual activity, makes him more vulnerable than a god-figure should be. After Damon's historic perfect game, Henry builds dramatic significance around his next pitching assignment, which holds the possibility of further perfection and thus even more historic importance. The day of the game is turned into Brock Rutherford Day, a tribute to Damon's father as the central figure in the history of the Association. But Henry's involvement goes much further than this. Both Henry and Brock are fifty-six years old, and their complete identification with the game-world is pointed up by the fact that the Association is also in its fifty-sixth season. Since Brock and Henry are the same age, and since Henry has always had both a deep admiration for Brock's skills and a profound respect for his values, the identification of Henry and Brock is almost complete. Since Damon is the son of Brock, Henry's affection toward Damon is fatherly: Damon, by extension, is, after all, the son of god. Damon's opponent in this central game is Jock Casey, another star rookie pticher, and one whose ancestry may be traced back to Fancy Dan Casey, one of the greats of Year I of the Association. The struggle between Damon and Casey thus has a doubly historic significance even before Henry turns the events of that game into ritual: there is the commemoration of the Brock Rutherford Era with Brock and all the great personages of his time in attendance; and there is the duel between Damon and Casey, with the possibility of extending Damon's perfect game into a second. As Henry muses before the game, "It was *more* than history, it was, it was: *fulfillment!*" (p. 52).

The introduction of death into the game is eventually positive because it makes the game more profound; it projects the game, and Henry's conception of the game, into a more serious stature by bridging the gap between the game and external reality. Coover is making the most direct challenge of any of the novelists in this study to the reader's tendency to dichotomize play and seriousness, game and reality, by portraying a game-world which becomes increasingly integrative and whole. The dice dictate that Damon is killed by one of Casey's pitches. Henry feels powerless to do anything about the gratuitous act of the dice, and so he invents a corresponding gratuitousness in Casey to account for his loss. Suddenly, Casey becomes a villain, who after shaking off several signs from his catcher, threw a pitch which he wanted to hit Damon. While Henry may arrange the circumstances of Damon's death and thus make them slightly more manageable, or superficially explicable, he is incapable of changing the verdict of the dice. Casey must therefore share the responsibility for Damon's death with the unthinking and heedless dice: "Oh, sure, he was free to throw away the dice, run the game by whim, but then what would be the point of it? Who would Damon Rutherford really be then? Nobody, an empty name, a play actor. Even though he'd set his own rules, his own limits, and though he could change them whenever he wished, nevertheless he and his players were committed to the turns of the mindless and unpredictable—one might even say, irresponsible—dice. . . . He had to accept it, or quit the game altogether" (pp. 34-35). Henry realizes that integrity is essential to the freedom of play. One might recall that what made the snow football game in *End Zone* so compelling was the free acceptance of rules which limited and defined the game. Henry understands that a violation of the rules destroys the play-attitude, the whole reality which is the game. His commitment to the game demands an adherence to its rules because the game is real to him and, like all play, has final consequences. Henry's response is therefore not that of a detached observer, but of an engaged and fatherly participant: "The Proprietor of the Universal Baseball Association, utterly brought down, brought utterly to grief, buried his face in the heap of papers on his kitchen table and cried for a long bad time" (p. 59). As Ehrmann had predicted, Henry has become both an object of his own play world as well as the subject of Coover's. The seriousness of Henry's response represents the profundity of his play-world. "Play cannot therefore be isolated as an activity without *consequences*. Its integrity, its gratuitousness are only apparent, since the very freedom of the expenditure made in it is part of a circuit which reaches beyond the spatial and temporal limits of play."[7]

The extent to which Damon's death reaches beyond the spatial and temporal limits of the Association is manifested in Henry's complete inability to function outside the play-world and the overwhelming influence which the Association begins to have on Henry's external relationships. At first Henry is so immobilized by Damon's death that he cannot bring himself to face the tiresome columns of figures he is responsible for at his accounting job. That evening he visits his friend and co-worker, Lou Engle, but before he actually arrives he is already imagining Lou's apartment as the scene of Damon's funeral. Lou's apartment is transformed in Henry's imagination into a musty Gothic cathedral. Lou infers that Henry is in mourning, never of course suspecting that the deceased is a player in a game-world, and he plays, at Henry's insistence, a series of classical recordings which should be appropriate for a funeral. But the intended solemnity of the occasion is crushed by irreverence. Henry becomes drunk, Lou is constantly bumping into things, including the record player, and the "players" Henry has assembled for the funeral are making fun of their creator's sentimentality. In the midst of a funeral piece by Purcell, Henry, drinking sherry, bourbon, and whiskey, turns the record player to a higher speed, and irreverently reduces the funeral to a shambles.

After the funeral, Coover further reinforces the play-world as real and serious by paraphrasing the most common of clichés about death with the diction of play. And so "Play resumed. It always resumes . . ." (p. 71). Play, like life, must go on. But the problem for Henry is *how* to go on. The order which once seemed so natural a part of the game has become a source of dread both for Henry and for the players in the Association. Sycamore Flynn, Casey's manager, thinks about calling off the rest of the season, but wonders "what would all the past mean then without the present process? Nothing at all, but so what? No answers: only dread. . . . Finally, he supposed, it would resume, and he would simply have to play out his part. But he dreaded that, too" (p. 88).

Above even Henry is the impersonal force of fate, physically represented by the dice, but more interestingly conceived of as Robert Coover. The coincidence of Casey killing Damon precisely on Brock Rutherford Day is an authorial machination, a contrivance designed to point up the limitations of Henry's commitment to the dice. Henry himself begins to see that commitment as a sign of his own impotence. He vows revenge on Casey, who increasingly comes to haunt his imagination, and around whom he builds an aura of rebelliousness and defiance. The very first description of Casey emphasizes that he "Played the game his own way, threw everything except what the catcher ordered, got along with no one . . ." (p. 52), and foreshadows Casey's killing Damon when he shakes off the catcher's signal twice before beaning his rival, then stands "oddly aloof" on the mound as Damon's teammates murderously charge him. When play resumes Casey's every move is unpredictable, some even contradict his manager's signals, but as if in defiance of Henry's will, everything Casey does is successful. Henry does everything in his power to defeat Casey: he even goes so far as to roll the dice for the first hitter before writing Casey's name into the lineup. But Henry's limited and partial measures are of little consequence. Casey continues to win ballgames and Henry walks the streets "possessed by impotence. . . . If he didn't know better, he'd suspect the dice of malevolence, rather than mere mindlessness. And it was Henry, not Casey, who was losing control" (pp. 111-12).

Henry sees his apparent loss of control as part of "the new and wearisome order" of the game. But the order of the game has not changed at all, only Henry's understanding of his increasing identification with the play-world and his personal involvement with its players. He tries to rationalize his growing sense of impotence in a meditation about Casey which once again shows the inseparability of the creator and his creation:

Impotent? not really. But sometimes total power was worse. Message of the Legalists: without law, power lost its shape. That was what kept Casey proud: born into a going system, he judged himself by it, failed to look beyond, look back: who said three strikes made an out? Supposing he just shipped Casey to the minors and to hell with the rules? He could at that. If he wanted to. Could explain it in the Book. It wasn't impotence. Still, it might cause trouble. What trouble? The players . . . What players? *Some* kind of limit there, all right, now that he thought about it. He might smash their resistance, but he couldn't help *feeling* that resistance all the same. Their? mine; it was all the same. [P. 115.]

Henry cannot in any meaningful way separate his own reality from that of the play-world. The order of the game—the rules of whimsy by which it is run—is just as relative as its ontology. In the monologue above, Henry begins to see himself as Coover has always intended the reader to see him: as both the subject and object of play, as player and toy, as creator and participant.

As a way of infusing new life and meaning into the game, as a way of restoring its faltering order, Henry attempts to share it with Lou Engel. But Lou only contributes to the further dissolution of the game and Henry's control of it, because he cannot possibly understand the magnitude of the creative act which produced the game in the first place. Since the play-world is a product of Henry's imagination—and Lou, of course, is not—Lou must be seen as an intruder. The play-world is a manifestation of the sacred, but Lou can only conceive of it in profane terms; he cannot, for example, imagine what Henry's stacks of paper (records, charts, the Book) have to do with a "mere" game. And while Henry approaches the play-sphere with respect, by washing his hands, Lou "absently" wipes *his* hands on his pants. Most importantly, however, Lou is still another example of the pragmatist figure who appears in all sports fiction. He approaches the game as a manipulator, interested only in those strategies which conduce to winning and not necessarily those in keeping with the spirit and integrity of the game. Lou is a quintessential example of what Robert E. Neale calls the "funster." His response to the play-world is "superficial because it avoids the heights and depths of life by attenuating human responses. And it is selfish because it uses other people for the sake of private pleasure. The funsters seek diversion from work, but the result is only diversion from life."[8] Lou's presence in the game proves to be truly disruptive. He cannot, or will not, understand the intricacies of strategy because he can *only* understand the game metaphor in terms of victory. He is, in Bernard Suits's terminology, a "trifler." Lou's intrusion into the game-world emphasizes that it is radically individualistic and cannot be shared. With his beer and pizza, Lou upsets the balance and order which make Henry's play world so vivid and real, and thus reinforces our sense that Henry's proprietorship over a play-world is an intensely lonely one.

The chaos which Lou brings to the game culminates in his spilling beer all over the Association and its records. With the game almost a complete shambles, Henry seriously and for the first time contemplates sacking it. But the magnitude of the power which Henry might use to destroy the game implies the godlike act which engendered it. Henry begins to see a way of saving the game, but only if he reasserts that power and transgresses the rules to which he has felt so committed. He realizes that all the seemingly chaotic influences on the game reduce to one central fact—Damon Rutherford is dead. The solution, in a word, is murder.

Henry cheats and changes 2-6-6 on the dice to 6-6-6 and thus moves the game over to the Extraordinary Occurrences Chart. Another roll of 6-6-6 would mean that Royce Ingram, the batter, would kill Casey, the pitcher, with a line drive. Henry has several, anxious second thoughts about the consequences of what he feels he must do: "Do you really *want* to save it? Wouldn't it be better just to drop it now, burn it, go on to something else, get working regularly again, back into the swing of things, see movies, maybe copyright that Intermonop game and try to market it, or do some traveling, read books . . ." (p. 144). None of the alternatives here is reasonable because none is as real and compelling as the Association. And so Henry murders Casey by controlling the dice instead of submitting to them. The horror of the act is appropriately emphasized by Henry's spasmodic vomiting which convulses him "with the impact of a smashing line drive . . ." (p. 145). Still, the implications of this scene go beyond the use of violence in any of the previously discussed sports fiction. Henry, acting as a participant-god in the play-sphere, has introduced murder as a means of saving the play-world. In *Fat City* and *North Dallas Forty*, the violence of the game is never seen as playful. It is pure hostility without any of the harmony essential to play. The snow football game in *End Zone* and playground basketball in *One on One* are examples of how violence may be tolerated in the play-world, perhaps even be made somehow essential to it. But murder? One is tempted to say, surely that is stretching the play metaphor too far. But murder is precisely the game point here. The ultimate posture of Coover's book is that the imaginative re-creation of the play-world has become the world—not the only world, but the most interesting and vital one for Henry Waugh. The separation of the play-world is complete in *The Universal Baseball Association*, not partial as it was in *One on One*. And once the play-world is seen as total, self-enclosed, one might properly ask, why not death? It gives that world still more completeness than even its creator—Waugh—had anticipated, but surely no less profundity than Waugh's creator intended the reader to see.

The self-sufficiency and completeness of Henry's Association are emphasized by the startling vision of the last chapter of the novel, in which the tragic deaths of Damon Rutherford and Jock Casey have been transmuted into the full mature play of ritual. Henry's violation of the rules of the game, his assertion of his superior personality, paradoxically confirms those rules and establishes the primacy of the game over his personality. The world of the Association has been sealed off: every character who appears in chapter 8 of *The Universal Baseball Association* is a descendant of a previous player. Perhaps the most striking aspect of the play-world here is that Henry Waugh has ceased to appear as a character. The harmony of play has evidently become so complete that there is not even enough conflict to ensure survival. Henry's identification with the Association is so total that, to paraphrase Robert E. Neale, all play and no work have made no Henry.[9] The imaginative re-creation of sport as play has become the world. There is not the slightest sign here of any other reality; even the existence of a creator external to the play-world may now only be inferred.

The subject of the last chapter is the annual reenactment of the Parable of the Duel. The Parable is a mythic condensation of the deaths of Damon and Casey into a single game, and each season the Association's top rookies must assume the roles of their forebears and play out the story. The ritual has distinctly religious overtones: it is played on Damonsday of each season, which, like Doomsday, is a day of judgment for the rookies, an initiation ceremony for each new crop of innocents. The events surrounding the Damon-Casey duel are now 101 seasons old, and so like all mythic stories the Parable of the Duel and its ritual enactment are subject to interpretation. Damon has come to represent the power of tradition and conservatism, an image which is foreshadowed very early in the novel when Henry identifies Damon's "total involvement, his one-ness with the Universal Baseball Association" (p. 13). Casey, the original villain in Henry's imagination, has become an existential hero whose "essential freedom" and "uniqueness" are emphasized by his partisans. The mythic Casey is also foreshadowed by earlier history: "He kept seeing Jock Casey, waiting there on the mound. Why waiting? Who for? Patient. Yes, give him credit, he was. Enduring. And you had to admit: Casey played the game, heart and soul. Played it like nobody had ever played it before. He circled round the man, viewing him from all angles. Lean, serious, melancholy even. And alone. Yes, above all: alone" (p. 145).

The Parable of the Duel must therefore be seen as the central myth of the Universal Baseball Association. The creation of a myth is essential to full mature play,[10] and so the Parable is also Henry's playful response to the threat of chaos in the play-sphere. Coover has foreshadowed the very idea of turning the history of the Association into myth even before Damon's death. He has Henry see with uncanny irony that the pitcher's duel between Damon and Casey is "Not just a duel of dynasties, but a *real* duel, a duel to the death between Jock Casey and Damon Ruther-ford . . ." (p. 55). Henry, clearly nervous about what for him is the real possibility of death, sees the two great rookie pitchers "waiting for this awful rite to be played out" (p. 55). And after Damon's death, Henry is already thinking about turning the fact into legend. The inspiration for treating Damon's death as folklore is prepared for as early as the post-funeral party at Jake's at which Sandy Shaw, folk-balladeer of the Associa-tion, creates a maudlin ballad about Damon's death to the tune of "Tom Dooley."

Rather than relying on some established tradition of myth as, for example, Malamud's use of the Grail legend and vegetation myths in *The Natural*, Coover allows Henry to find a new order for his play-world by literally creating his own myth out of the history of that world. Given the overwhelming concern with history, order, and process in the Association, the Parable of the Duel as myth and ritual seems natural. Henry is impli-cated in Casey's death; his personal involvement in the play-world makes him guilty of murder. The transformation of history into myth provides the distance necessary to mitigate and contain the crime. It allows for a playful response to climactic events which must be transcended to main-tain order, but which, also to maintain continuity in the play-world, may not be excluded.

What *is* excluded from the play world is anything that is not essential to it. The initial movement of the novel was to pose a dualism between the literal world of Dunklemann, Zauber and Zifferblatt, the realm of work; and the imaginative and playful sphere of Henry's Association. But by the last chapter of the novel, the low-mimetic world of accounting firms has vanished; it simply does not exist any more. The only world that exists is the one that has been imaginatively re-created. The separa-tion of this world is so total that it has finally given rise to its own dualism: the players in the Association are now trying to distinguish between the reality of their own world and the ritual they are about to perform, a play-form within the play-world. The conflict necessary to ensure survival no longer comes from Henry's vacillation between two worlds but from within the play-world itself.

The source of that conflict is epitomized by the ritual, the meaning of which is unclear since over 100 seasons have elapsed since the original Damon-Casey duel. There are those like Cuss McCamish who treat the ritual with profanity. McCamish goes so far as to suggest irreverently that Casey, like Christ, returns in the flesh each year to act his part in the ritual. However, the profaners are all characters who think their roles in the ritual will not personally involve them in the tragedy and so they feel removed from the central action of the rite. Others, like Paul Trench and Hardy Ingram, who must play the roles of Royce Ingram and Damon Rutherford, are deeply troubled by the potential consequences of their participation. Hardy Ingram is actually a Caseyite and cannot believe that by some ironic twist he must play the role of Damon Rutherford. Yet he has a vivid premonition of the reality and truth of his role, a premonition which is pointed up when he "feels a tingling just behind his left ear" (p. 160). Skeeter Parsons advises Hardy in all earnestness to step back from the fatal pitch when it comes: "Maybe . . . maybe, Hardy, they're gonna kill you out there today!" (p. 163). Hardy curses in response, but his gruffness is clearly a way of hiding his fear. Once again he "feels a cold chill rattle through him, tingling that patch behind his ear . . ." (pp. 163-64).

Paul Trench, who must play the role of the Avenger, is so anxious about his participation that he is led to the following rumination: "He wants to quit—but what does he mean, 'quit'? The game? Life? Could you separate them?" (p. 171). The answer is clearly "No." But the dread which Trench feels is in keeping with the character of all sacred rites. As Huizinga points out, "The function of the rite . . . is far from being merely imitative; it causes the worshippers to participate in the sacred happening itself."[11]

Indeed, the self-enclosed, mythic play-world at the end of *The Universal Baseball Association* has all the characteristics which Huizinga identified as essential to play: joy, creativity, freedom, tension, and isolation. Huizinga's only major error, and the one which later play theorists have continually taken him to task for, is his failure to see that play, while it may be separated from the literal world, may never be divorced from its potential consequences. He failed to see that there is no necessary dichotomy between play and seriousness or play and reality.

Henry Waugh's Universal Baseball Association is the ultimate re-creation of sport because it becomes the world. For the first time one sees that the risks implied by the spirit of adventure are real; play may be so compelling that the adventurer transcends not only self-consciousness but self. Unlike

Elwood Baskin, even, Henry Waugh is not merely central to his play-world, he *is* the play-world and all its players simultaneously. He is schizophrenic, but he is god. "Full play by the mature adult can be understood as the end goal of human development. Obviously such an experience is quite rare. . . . But the ultimate experience does occur, and when it does, although it is similar to all the partial adventures that have preceded it, it is of such greater breadth as to seem entirely different. And the experience is labeled as it has always been labeled—it is called 'holy.'"[12]

The final vision of the eighth chapter is strikingly indeterminate. There are no final answers for the players in the game world, for even the mythic order of the Association is only one possibility among many. As Hardy Ingram says of the ritual, "It's not a trial. . . . It's not even a lesson. It's just what it is" (p. 174). The ritual is not played out; a ninth chapter would have implied the perfection of a completed baseball game, an orderliness and tidiness which the novel argues can never be absolute. What makes the Association universal, the only absolute in the game-world, is the play-attitude. Play encompasses the joy, creativity, and freedom which engendered the Association; play produced the story which became its central myth; and play is the essence of ritual, through which the myth is acted out. The Universal Baseball Association is the most supremely playful imaginative re-creation of sport, and, since it is mythic, and thus timeless, it partakes not so much of "real time" as "significant time" (p. 155).

NOTES

1. PLAYFUL FICTIONS AND FICTIONAL PLAYERS

1. René Maheu, "Sport and Culture," in *Sport and American Society*, ed. George H. Sage (London: Addison-Wesley, 1970), pp. 386-87.

2. Aside from the novels in this study, some of the more interesting and prominent examples of recent sports fiction include the following: William Brashler, *The Bingo Long Travelling All Stars and Motor Kings* (1973); Jerome Charyn, *The Seventh Babe* (1979); James Dickey, *Deliverance* (1971); Frederick Exley, *A Fan's Notes* (1968); Peter Gent, *Texas Celebrity Turkey Trot* (1978); Robert Greenfield, *Haymon's Crowd* (1978); Mark Harris, *It Seemed Like Forever* (1979, the fourth volume in the tetralogy that begins with *The Southpaw* and *Bang the Drum Slowly*); Paul Hemphill, *Long Gone* (1979); John Irving, *The 158-Pound Marriage* (1974); Sam Koperwas, *Westchester Bull* (1976); Jay Neugeboren, *Big Man* (1966) and *Sam's Legacy* (1975); Philip F. O'Connor, *Stealing Home* (1979); Philip Roth, *The Great American Novel* (1973); James Salter, *Solo Faces* (1979); John Sayles, *Pride of the Bimbos* (1975); Patricia Nell Warren, *The Front Runner* (1974); and James Whitehead, *Joiner* (1971).

3. Johan Huizinga, *Homo Ludens* (1950; rpt. Boston: Beacon Press, 1955), p. 1.

4. Eugen Fink, "The Oasis of Happiness: Toward an Ontology of Play," *Yale French Studies*, 41 (1968), 22.

5. Erik H. Erikson, *Childhood and Society* (New York: W. W. Norton & Company, Inc., 1963), p. 222.

6. David L. Miller, summarizing the Swiss psychologist Jean Piaget, in *Gods and Games: Toward a Theology of Play* (1970; rpt. New York: Harper Colophon Books, 1973), p. 122.

7. Miller, p. 123.

8. Allen Guttmann, *From Ritual to Record: The Nature of Modern Sports* (New York: Columbia University Press, 1978), p. 4.

9. The idea of games as models for succeeding over others is discussed by Brian Sutton-Smith and John M. Roberts in "The Cross-Cultural and Psychological Study of Games," in *The Cross-Cultural Analysis of Sport and Games*, ed. Gunther Luschen (Champaign, Illinois: Stipes, 1970), pp. 100-107.

10. Jacques Ehrmann, "Homo Ludens Revisited," *Yale French Studies*, 41 (1968), 41.

11. Huizinga, pp. 5, 8.

12. Huizinga, p. 9.
13. Roger Caillois, "Toward a Sociology derived from Games," in Sage, p. 368.
14. Ehrmann, p. 55.
15. Ehrmann, p. 56.
16. Robert E. Neale, *In Praise of Play: Toward a Psychology of Religion* (New York: Harper & Row, 1969), p. 24.
17. Fink, p. 22.
18. Huizinga, p. 45.
19. Miller, p. 6.
20. Ehrmann, p. 55.
21. Arnold Beisser, "Modern Man and Sports," in *Sport and Society: An Anthology*, eds. John T. Talamini and Charles H. Page (Boston: Little, Brown, 1973), p. 96.
22. Howard S. Slusher, *Man, Sport, and Existence* (Philadelphia: Lea & Febiger, 1967), p. 181.
23. Paul Weiss, *Sport: A Philosophic Inquiry* (Carbondale: Southern Illinois University Press, Arcturus Books edition, 1971), p. 14.
24. Beisser, p. 95.
25. Murray Ross, "Football and Baseball in America," in Talamini and Page, p. 102.
26. Quoted by John Loy, "The Nature of Sport: A Definitional Effort," in M. Marie Hart, *Sport in the Socio-Cultural Process* (1st ed., Dubuque: William C. Brown, 1972), p. 62.

2. IRONIC DETERMINISM IN *FAT CITY*

1. Eugen Fink, "The Oasis of Happiness: Toward an Ontology of Play," *Yale French Studies*, 41 (1968), 25.
2. Robert E. Neale, *In Praise of Play: Toward a Psychology of Religion* (New York: Harper & Row, 1969), p. 53.
3. Fink, pp. 24-25.
4. All page references are to the first edition, Farrar, Straus and Giroux: New York, 1969.
5. Neale, p. 96.
6. Neale, p. 96.
7. Arnold Beisser, "Modern Man and Sports," in *Sport and Society: An Anthology*, eds. John T. Talamini and Charles H. Page (Boston: Little, Brown, 1973), p. 93
8. Howard S. Slusher, *Man, Sport, and Existence* (Philadelphia: Lea & Febiger, 1967), p. 35.
9. Nathan Hare, "The Occupational Culture of the Black Fighter," in *Sport and Society: An Anthology*, eds. John T. Talamini and Charles H. Page (Boston: Little, Brown, 1973), pp. 315-17.
10. Hare, p. 318. Hare is relying here on a study made by S. Kirson Weinberg and Henry Arond published as "The Occupational Culture of the Boxer," *American Journal of Sociology*, March, 1952, p. 460.

3. *NORTH DALLAS FORTY*: Professionalism and the Corruption of Play

1. Howard S. Slusher, *Man, Sport and Existence* (Philadelphia: Lea & Febiger, 1967), p. 134.
2. Murray Ross, "Football and Baseball in America," in *Sport and Society: An Anthology*, eds. John T. Talamini and Charles H. Page, (Boston: Little, Brown, 1973), pp. 102-12. Several of the remarks below which attempt to describe a mythos of football show an indebtedness to Ross's brilliant essay.

3. Quoted in Paul Hoch's *Rip Off the Big Game* (Garden City, New York: Doubleday Anchor Books, 1972), p. 8.
4. Hoch, p. 10.
5. Johan Huizinga, *Homo Ludens* (1950; rpt. Boston: Beacon, 1955), p. 13.
6. Paul Weiss, *Sport: A Philosophical Inquiry* (Carbondale: Southern Illinois University Press, Arcturus Books edition, 1971), p. 137.
7. Erik H. Erikson, *Childhood and Society* (New York: W. W. Norton & Company, Inc., 1963), p. 212.
8. Erikson, p. 212.
9. All page references are to the following edition: New York: William Morrow & Company, 1973.
10. Just how compelling and truly playful a really essential form of football might be will be discussed in the next chapter in connection with the snow football game in *End Zone*.
11. Slusher, p. 4.
12. Eugen Fink, "The Oasis of Happiness: Toward an Ontology of Play," *Yale French Studies*, 41 (1968), 23.
13. Slusher, p. 4.
14. Slusher, p. 4.
15. David L. Miller, *Gods and Games: Toward a Theology of Play* (New York: Harper Colophon, 1970), p. 174.
16. Huizinga, p. 89.
17. Huizinga, p. 89.
18. Dick Schaap, review of *North Dallas Forty* in *New York Times Book Review*, Oct. 28, 1973, p. 44.
19. Hoch, p. 10.
20. Allen Guttmann, *From Ritual to Record: The Nature of Modern Sports* (New York: Columbia University Press, 1978), p. 133.

4. *END ZONE*: Play at the Brink

1. Murray Ross, "Football and Baseball in America," in *Sport and Society: An Anthology*, eds. John T. Talamini and Charles H. Page, (Boston: Little, Brown, 1973), p. 107.
2. Ross, p. 110.
3. Roger Caillois, *Man and the Sacred*, trans. Meyer Barash (Glencoe, Illinois: The Free Press, 1959), p. 161.
4. Johan Huizinga, *Homo Ludens: A Study of the Play Element in Culture* (1950; rpt. Boston: Beacon, 1955), p. 89.
5. Huizinga, p. 210.
6. All page references are to the Pocket Books edition, April, 1973.
7. Eugen Fink, "The Oasis of Happiness: Toward an Ontology of Play," *Yale French Studies*, 41 (1968), 23.
8. Jacques Ehrmann, "Homo Ludens Revisited," *Yale French Studies*, 41 (1968), 55.
9. Fink, p. 22.
10. Huizinga, p. 129.
11. Robert E. Neale, *In Praise of Play: Toward a Psychology of Religion* (New York: Harper and Row, 1969), p. 24.
12. Neale, p. 120.
13. Huizinga, p. 122.
14. Mircea Eliade, *The Sacred and the Profane: The Nature of Religion*, trans. Willard R. Trask (New York: Harvest, 1959), p. 10. Eliade uses this as an "initial" definition which is made specific by the rest of his inquiry.
15. Huizinga, p. 21.

16. According to Huizinga, there is no play-attitude in intercourse itself: "it would be erroneous to incorporate the sexual act itself, as love-play, in the play category" (Huizinga, p. 43). I think Huizinga is undoubtedly wrong about "love-play," but Delillo's emphasis on foreplay leaves no doubt about *his* intentions.
17. Neale, p. 24.
18. Neale, p. 24.
19. Huizinga, p. 15.
20. Huizinga, p. 28.
21. Neale, p. 25.
22. Neale, p. 25.
23. Neale, p. 104.
24. Neale, p. 104.

5. *ONE ON ONE*: Zen and the Art of Basketball

1. I have borrowed the term from Gregory P. Stone, who uses it to describe the self-serving spectacle in sport, "American Sports: Play and Display," in *Sport and Society: An Anthology*, ed. John T. Talamini and Charles H. Page (Boston: Little, Brown, 1973).
2. All page references are to the first edition, New York: Holt, Rinehart, and Winston, 1970.
3. Robert E. Neale, *In Praise of Play: Toward a Psychology of Religion* (New York: Harper & Row, 1969), p. 111.
4. Johan Huizinga, *Homo Ludens* (1950; rpt. Boston: Beacon, 1955), p. 10.
5. Huizinga, p. 10.
6. Pete Axthelm, "The City Game," in *Sport in the Socio-Cultural Process*, ed. M. Marie Hart (1st edition, Dubuque: William C. Brown, 1972), p. 188.
7. Kostas Axelos, "An Introduction to Planetary Thought," *Yale French Studies*, 41 (1968), 7.
8. David L. Miller, *Gods and Games: Toward a Theology of Play* (New York: Harper & Row, Harper Colophon, 1973), pp. 103-4.
9. Neale, p. 120.
10. Neale, p. 111.
11. Howard S. Slusher, *Man, Sport and Existence* (Philadelphia: Lea & Febiger, 1967), p. 127.
12. Eugen Fink, "The Oasis of Happiness: Toward an Ontology of Play," *Yale French Studies*, 41 (1968), 20.
13. Fink, p. 23.
14. René Maheu, "Sport and Culture," in *Sport and American Society*, ed. George H. Sage, (London: Addison-Wesley, 1970), p. 390.
15. Slusher, pp. 126-27.
16. Bill Bradley, *Life on the Run* (New York: Bantam, 1977), p. 172.
17. Axthelm, p. 188.
18. Fink, p. 21.
19. This is a paraphrase of R. D. Laing's definition of schizophrenia in *The Politics of Experience* (New York: Ballantine Books, 1967). The entire relevant passage is quoted below:

. . . it seems to us *without exception* the experience and behavior that gets labeled schizophrenic is a *special strategy that a person invents in order to live in an unlivable situation*. In his life situation the person has come to feel he is in an untenable position. He cannot make a move, or make no move, without being beset by contradictory and paradoxical pressures and demands, pushes and pulls, both internally from himself, and externally from those around him. He is, as it were, in a position of checkmate. [Pp. 114-15.]

It is not my intention to provide a psychoanalytical reading of the novel or of Elwood's schizoid experience. The novel can surely be read as a parody of the conventions and jargon of psychiatry and psychoanalysis, but except insofar as that jargon is antithetical to a playful and expressive language, those readings are not really to the point here. The passage has been quoted at length because I think Laing's conception of schizophrenia, here and in *The Divided Self*, is helpful in perceiving Elwood's experience.

6. THE UNIVERSAL BASEBALL ASSOCIATION: Play as Personalized Myth

1. Eugen Fink, "The Oasis of Happiness: Toward an Ontology of Play," *Yale French Studies*, 41 (1968), 24-25.
2. Quoted in Howard S. Slusher, *Man, Sport, and Existence* (Philadelphia: Lea & Febiger, 1967), p. 9.
3. All page references are to the Signet edition, New York: New American Library, 1969.
4. Kostas Axelos, "An Introduction to Planetary Thought," *Yale French Studies*, 41 (1968), 9.
5. Robert E. Neale, *In Praise of Play: Toward a Psychology of Religion* (New York: Harper & Row, 1969), p. 172.
6. Jacques Ehrmann, "Homo Ludens Revisited," *Yale French Studies*, 41 (1968), 55.
7. Ehrmann, pp. 42-43.
8. Neale, pp. 172-73.
9. Neale, p. 104.
10. See Robert E. Neale, "Full mature play creates the type of story defined as myth" (p. 135).
11. Johan Huizinga, *Homo Ludens* (1950; rpt. Boston: Beacon, 1955), p. 15.
12. Neale, p. 86.

SELECT BIBLIOGRAPHY

Axelos, Kostas. "Planetary Interlude." *Yale French Studies*, 41 (1968), 6-18.
Axthelm, Pete. "The City Game." *Sport in the Socio-Cultural Process.* Ed. M. Marie Hart. Dubuque: William C. Brown, 1972, pp. 187-205.
Beisser, Arnold. "The American Seasonal Masculinity Rites." *Sport in the Socio-Cultural Process.* Ed. M. Marie Hart. Dubuque: William C. Brown, 1972, pp. 259-68.
– – –. "Modern Man and Sports." *Sport and Society: An Anthology.* Eds. John T. Talamini and Charles H. Page. Boston: Little, Brown, 1973, pp. 85-96.
Bradley, Bill. *Life on the Run.* 1976; rpt. New York: Bantam Books, 1977.
Browne, Evelyn. "An Ethological Theory of Play." *Sport and American Society: Selected Readings.* Ed. George H. Sage. Reading, Massachusetts: Addison-Wesley, 1970, pp. 368-75.
Bruner, Jerome S., Alison Jolly, and Kathy Sylva, eds. *Play: Its Role in Development and Evolution.* New York: Basic Books, 1976.
Caillois, Roger. *Man and the Sacred.* Trans. Meyer Barash. Glencoe, Illinois: Free Press, 1959.
– – –. *Man, Play, and Games.* Trans. Meyer Barash. Glencoe, Illinois: Free Press, 1961.
Caplan, Frank and Theresa. *The Power of Play.* New York: Doubleday paperback, 1974.
Denney, Reuel. "The Spectatorial Forms." *Sport and Society: An Anthology.* Eds. John T. Talamini and Charles H. Page. Boston: Little, Brown, 1973, pp. 380-93.
Ehrmann, Jacques, ed. *Game, Play, Literature. Yale French Studies*, 41 (1968).
– – –. "Homo Ludens Revisited." *Yale French Studies*, 41 (1968), 31-57.
Eliade, Mircea. *The Sacred and the Profane: The Nature of Religion.* Trans. Willard R. Trask. New York: Harcourt, Brace & World, 1959.
Erikson, Erik H. *Childhood and Society.* 2nd ed., revised and enlarged. New York: Norton, 1963.
– – –. *Toys and Reasons: Stages in the Ritualization of Experience.* New York: Norton, 1977.
Fink, Eugen. "The Oasis of Happiness: Toward an Ontology of Play." *Yale French Studies,* 41 (1968), 19-30.
Guttman, Allen. *From Ritual to Record: The Nature of Modern Sports.* New York: Columbia University Press, 1978.

Hare, Nathan. "The Occupational Culture of the Black Fighter." *Sport and Society*: *An Anthology*. Eds. John T. Talamini and Charles H. Page. Boston: Little, Brown, 1973, pp. 315-25.

Hart, M. Marie, ed. *Sport in the Socio-Cultural Process*. Dubuque: William C. Brown, 1972.

— — —. *Sport in the Socio-Cultural Process*. 2nd ed., Dubuque: William C. Brown, 1976.

Hoch, Paul. *Rip Off the Big Game: The Exploitation of Sports by the Power Elite*. Garden City, New York: Doubleday, 1972.

Huizinga, Johan. *Homo Ludens: A Study of the Play-Element in Culture*. 1950; rpt. Boston: Beacon Press, 1955.

Lahr, John. "The Theatre of Sports." *Sport in the Socio-Cultural Process*. Ed. M. Marie Hart. Dubuque: William C. Brown, 1972, pp. 105-15.

Laing, R. D. *The Divided Self: An Existential Study in Sanity and Madness*. Middlesex, England: Penguin, 1965.

Leonard, George. *The Ultimate Athlete: Re-Visioning Sports, Physical Education, and the Body*. 1975; rpt. New York: Avon Books, 1977.

Lowe, Benjamin. *The Beauty of Sport*. Englewood Cliffs, New Jersey: Prentice-Hall, 1977.

Loy, John W., Jr. "The Nature of Sport: A Definitional Effort." *Sport in the Socio-Cultural Process*. Ed. M. Marie Hart. Dubuque: William C. Brown, 1972, pp. 50-66.

Luschen, Gunther, ed. *The Cross-Cultural Analysis of Sport and Games*. Champaign: Stipes, 1970.

— — —. "The Interdependence of Sport and Culture." *Sport in the Socio-Cultural Process*. Ed. M. Marie Hart. Dubuque: William C. Brown, 1972, pp. 22-35.

Maheu, René. "Sport and Culture." *Sport and American Society: Selected Readings*. Ed. George H. Sage. Reading, Massachusetts: Addison-Wesley, 1970, pp. 386-97.

McLuhan, Marshall. "Games: The Extensions of Man." *Sport in the Socio-Cultural Process*. Ed. M. Marie Hart. Dubuque: William C. Brown, 1972, pp. 145-54.

Millar, Susanna. *The Psychology of Play*. Middlesex, England: Penguin, 1968.

Miller, David L. *Gods and Games: Toward a Theology of Play*. 1970; rpt. New York: Harper Colophon Edition, 1973.

Mumford, Lewis. "Sport and the 'Bitch-Goddess.'" *Sport and Society: An Anthology*. Eds. John T. Talamini and Charles H. Page. Boston: Little, Brown, 1973, pp. 60-64.

Neale, Robert E. *In Praise of Play: Toward a Psychology of Religion*. New York: Harper & Row, 1969.

Novak, Michael. *The Joy of Sports: End Zones, Bases, Baskets, Balls, and the Consecration of the American Spirit*. New York: Basic Books, 1976.

Osterhoudt, Robert G., ed. *The Philosophy of Sport: A Collection of Original Essays*. Springfield, Illinois: Charles C. Thomas, 1973.

Riesman, David, and Reuel Denney. "Football in America: A Study in Culture Diffusion." *Sport in the Socio-Cultural Process*. Ed. M. Marie Hart. Dubuque: William C. Brown, 1972, pp. 206-21.

Roberts, John M., et al. "Games in Culture." *Sport and American Society: Selected Readings*. Ed. George H. Sage. Reading, Massachusetts: Addison-Wesley, 1970, pp. 376-85.

Ross, Murray. "Football and Baseball in America." *Sport and Society: An Anthology*. Eds. John T. Talamini and Charles H. Page. Boston: Little, Brown, 1973, pp. 102-11.

Roszak, Theodore. "Forbidden Games." *Sport in the Socio-Cultural Process*. Ed. M. Marie Hart. Dubuque: William C. Brown, 1972, pp. 91-104.

Sage, George H., ed. *Sport and American Society: Selected Readings*. Reading, Massachusetts: Addison-Wesley, 1970.

Schmitz, Kenneth L. "Sport and Play: Suspension of the Ordinary." *Sport in the Socio-Cultural Process*. 2nd ed., Dubuque: William C. Brown, 1976, pp. 35-48.

Slusher, Howard S. *Man, Sport, and Existence: A Critical Analysis.* Philadelphia: Lea & Febiger, 1967.

Stone, Gregory P. "American Sports: Play and Display." *Sport and Society: An Anthology.* Eds. John T. Talamini and Charles H. Page. Boston: Little, Brown, 1973, pp. 65–84.

– – –. "Some Meanings of American Sport: An Extended View," *Sport in the Socio-Cultural Process.* Ed. M. Marie Hart. Dubuque: William C. Brown, 1972, pp. 155–67.

Suits, Bernard. *The Grasshopper: Games, Life and Utopia.* Toronto: University of Toronto Press, 1978.

Sutton-Smith, Brian, and John M. Roberts. "The Cross-Cultural and Psychological Study of Games." *The Cross-Cultural Analysis of Sport and Games.* Ed. Gunther Luschen. Champaign: Stipes, 1970.

Szasz, Thomas S., M.D. *The Myth of Mental Illness: Foundations of a Theory of Personal Conduct.* New York: Dell, 1961.

Talamini, John T. and Charles H. Page, eds. *Sport and Society: An Anthology.* Boston: Little, Brown, 1973.

Weiss, Paul. *Sport: A Philosophic Inquiry.* Carbondale: Southern Illinois University Press, 1971.

INDEX